THE IMA AND POETRY OF LUCRETIUS

David West

First published in 1969 by Edinburgh University Press
This edition first published in 1994 by
Bristol Classical Press
an imprint of
Gerald Duckworth & Co. Ltd
The Old Piano Factory
48 Hoxton Square, London N1 6PB

A catalogue record for this book is available
from the British Library

ISBN 1-85399-380-8

Printed in Great Britain by
The Cromwell Press, Melksham, Wiltshire

Contents

Still for Pamela

Preface

In reading poetry it pays to attend to the metaphors. This is true even in English where many of the metaphors are dead (like 'pays' and 'dead'). It is even truer in Latin which has a much livelier sense of the literal. There is still a problem, particularly with single words. Weight, for instance, is surely not important in the first line of the fourth book of the *Aeneid*, where Dido is said, literally, to be 'wounded by a *heavy* care', but when the literal force of a word is supported by another in the immediate context, the alert reader should respond. So these first two lines of *Aeneid* 4 have at least two live metaphors mixed, wounding and nourishment, as *saucia*, 'wounded', speaks to *vulnus*, and *alit* speaks to *carpitur*:

> At regina gravi iamdudum saucia cura
> volnus alit venis et caeco carpitur igni.
> *But the queen had long been suffering from the grief of love,*
> *feeding the wound in her veins and consumed by its hidden fire.*

This is a simple and obvious procedure, but in the 1960s when I was working on Lucretius, translators and commentators often failed to apply it. For this young man in those distant days it opened up a great deal of poetry, particularly the work of the three great metaphorical poets of Latin, Plautus, Lucretius and Horace, and this reprint goes out in the hope that this way of thinking may even now have a similar inspiriting effect on people coming to read poetry in which metaphor is important. This is a straight reprint of the 1969 edition. An appendix has been added giving some examples of possible future lines of advance in Lucretian studies.

In the quarter of a century since this book was written a great deal of work has been done on Lucretius. The best introduction is still Kenney's 48-page pamphlet invaluable for its sanity, economy and the just warmth of its response to the poet. A useful aid is Smith's revision of the Loeb translation with its running summary and brief notes. As always commentaries are essential for those who wish to make progress. The greatest achievement is R.D. Brown's massive edition of 4.1030-287 with its 143 pages of powerful prolegomena. Kenney has again served Lucretius brilliantly by his inexhaustibly informative commentary on book 3 and there are helpful editions by P.M. Brown, Godwin and Costa of books 1, 4 and 5. Substantial advances in our understanding of the Epicurean philosophy which Lucretius is teaching are charted in Long and Sedley's bibliography. Notable is the work of Clay, who makes a subtle and determined attempt to deduce the Lucretian colour in Lucretius' exposition of Epicurus. Classen has studied Lucretius' techniques of argument, a subject which I tackled much more narrowly in an article in *CQ*. Classen also edited an invaluable collection of research papers on Lucretius.

In the areas covered by this book Kenney (1970) is most illuminating on Lucretius' tendency to mimic his adversaries, a resource touched upon above in chapter 3. Relevant to chapter 8 are works by Snyder on puns and Dionigi on word play, but these subjects are not yet exhausted and both of these authors seem to me to fall into an error. In brief, Lucretius argues that the same atoms, arranged in different order, produce different entities just as the same letters in different order produce words with different meanings, as discussed on pages 24-5 and 97 below. Snyder, Dionigi, and other scholars start from the observation that the same letters can be parts of words of *similar* meaning. This opens the door to large collections of material, but also to misinterpretations of Lucretius' poetic and of the Atomic Theory, as suggested in my reviews in 1982 and 1991. At a detailed level the most interesting criticism has been by Gottschalk on my treatment of 1.974-83 on pages 47-8 above.

Details of all these works are given at the end of the appendix.

Introduction

Lucretius was an Epicurean. The principal aim of Epicu-
reans was peace of mind. In writing the *De Rerum Natura*,
Lucretius' principal aim was to save men from the superstitious fears and political ambitions which could destroy
that peace, and the instrument of salvation was a materialist
philosophy. The gods had not made the world, nor did they
interfere in it by acceding to our requests nor by punishing
us in this life or in the hereafter. There is no hereafter. We
and the world in which we live are shifting aggregations of
imperceptibly minute atoms falling endlessly through
empty space, hence for each of us death is the end, as our
component atoms move on to form new alliances. The *De
Rerum Natura* is a scientific treatise, expounding this
atomic theory with reference to everything about us from
the minutest of our perceptions to meteorological phenomena. This purely materialist philosophy achieves the prime
ethical purpose. The Epicurean studies physics solely in
order to free the mind from fear.

Out of this physics Lucretius built the greatest poem in
Latin, neglected by scholars writing in English, and in
large measure not understood.

This book is an attempt to provide an introduction to the
poetry of it, suggesting what it is in Lucretius that I find
magnificent. This, of course, can only be partial and personal, and my particular response is mainly to the images.
My basic procedure has been to point out the literal force
of Lucretius' metaphors where this has been ignored by
commentators and altered by translators. When I mention
these shortcomings, this is not purely pedantic malice. I am
trying to establish the present state of our understanding
of Lucretius in order to clarify my own suggestions and to
justify me in putting them forward. These new interpreta-

tions of detail have been so arranged that they illustrate and explore general characteristics of Lucretius' imagery and poetry, and I have always been ready to take my eyes off the main line of argument to examine the incidental splendours of the poetry; the images have not been fully listed and categorized into their subject matter, as they are in Sullwold's dissertation; nor have I carefully distinguished similes, metaphors, analogies and allegories, nor even mentioned symbolism; the philosophy I have taken as it comes, subordinating it to the elucidation of the poetry in a way that would have exasperated Lucretius. My only explanation of these weaknesses is that I have little interest in such distinctions, and that I have with appropriate fanaticism sacrificed everything to what I wanted to do – to advance the understanding and enjoyment of the poetry. Sir Roger Mynors, Mr J.Y. Nadeau and Dr P.G. Walsh have read the manuscript and made many valuable suggestions and excisions.

I have kept the text and punctuation of Martin's fourth edition (1959) except at 1 66, 118, 257, 657, 724, 928, 981; 2 672-3, 928-9; 4 79, 532, 544-5, 923; 6 896.

In the text, modern authors are referred to only by their surnames. Full details can be found at the end of the book in the bibliography.

1. The Importance of the Imagery and the Neglect of it

When Shakespeare in Sonnet 73 talks of bare ruined choirs, where late the sweet birds sang, we wonder if he means that he can no longer write poetry; we see the resemblance between the tracery of the branches of winter trees and the tracery of the windows of a ruined church; we feel the gloom and desolation of both scenes. Mind, sense and feeling are all engaged in complex activity. The same triple activity occurs when Pindar urges Hieron's son in *Pythian* 1 87-88 to forge his tongue on the anvil of truth, 'Any small spark which shoots out will fly with great force, since it is from you', and when Aeschylus in *Agamemnon* 437-44 sees the war god as 'a gold-changer of corpses, holding his scales in the spear fight and sending home to the loved ones from the fires of Troy heavy dust for them to weep over; instead of men, ashes stowed conveniently away in urns'.

No Latin poet can vie with Aeschylus, Pindar, or Shakespeare in complexity and daring in the use of imagery. But in Horace many images are rich by any standard; and for sublimity and passion, the imagery of Lucretius is unsurpassed. This being so it is surprising how commentators and translators ignore or traduce this vital element in the poetry. Admittedly it is not always easy to write usefully about something as fleeting and feeling as the effect of a poetic image. Before we can explore the 'bare ruined choirs', even as briefly as in the first sentence of this book, the reading voice has moved on to the next step in the argument, to a different image. The critic lumbers along behind, picking up the points of resemblance, scrutinizing them, and sug-gesting how the emotional colour of the images tinges the fundamental statement. This is analytical and subjective, but surely the commentator should explain the reference of the image if it is at all elusive, and surely the translator should not obscure it? The imagery is a precious part of the poetry and there is no sense in wasting it.

In Sonnet 65 Shakespeare asks what chance of survival has beauty, 'whose action is no stronger than a flower', when even steel and stone are liable to decay; and answers that it has none unless it survive in poetry. Poetry, monuments and flowers: these three terms come together in the same way in Lucretius, where he is refuting the notion that there were great wars before the Trojan war, that brave men lived before Agamemnon:

cur supera bellum Thebanum et funera Troiae
non alias alii quoque res cecinere poetae?
quo tot facta uirum totiens cecidere neque usquam
aeternis famae monimentis insita florent?
    5 326-9

Why did other poets not sing of other events before the Theban war and the bloodshed at Troy? Where have all these many heroic deeds fallen away to? Have they never been grafted on to the eternal monuments of fame to flower there?

When men erect monuments they are grafting their deeds on to a durable stock, the eternal monuments of fame, in this case poetry. This is full of poetry, including the juxta-position of stone and flower, the fragility of fame and flower, the seeming durability of monuments, the immor-tality of poetry, and man's elaborate operations to procure immortality for himself. All these pathetic sensations and meditations are floating through the Shakespeare and the Lucretius, and in Lucretius the literal force of the word *insita* is essential to it all. It is because they were never grafted that the prepoetic achievements of man are not in flower but have fallen to the ground. The translators offer 'enshrined in glory', 'set glorious', 'gravées', and 'blühn sie nicht fort'. This is murder.[1]

Another typical murder is done in the prologue to the third book:

hasce secundum res animi natura uidetur
atque animae claranda meis iam uersibus esse,
et metus ille foras praeceps Acheruntis agendus,
funditus humanam qui uitam turbat ab imo
omnia suffundens mortis nigrore neque ullam
esse uoluptatem liquidam puramque relinquit.

3 35-40

After this I must now make clear in my verses the nature of mind and soul and drive headlong out the old fear of Acheron which stirs up human life from the very bottom suffusing everything with the blackness of death and leaving no pleasure clear and pure.

Here Lucretius is obviously thinking of a clear pool or well with black mud at the bottom of it. *Funditus . . . turbat ab imo*, 'stirs up from the very bottom', is unmistakable; but Bailey mistakes it, 'utterly confounds the life of men from the very root'. In this version 'utterly' is wrong, 'confounds' is wrong, and 'from the very root' is monstrous. The Penguin translation by R.E. Latham, which is normally more sensitive than Bailey's, is on this occasion just as obtuse, 'blasting the life of man from its very foundations'. Translators are equally blind to the expressive word *suffundens*, suggesting the rising of the mud, and most of them indulge in 'unalloyed' pleasures in line 40, although this metallurgy is false to the Latin and destructive of the proper metaphor. Trevelyan, Diels, Ernout and even Munro spoil this passage. The Loeb translation by W.H.D. Rouse is the only one I have looked at which respects the Latin.[2]

Another passage will show in brief how vital the imagery is to our understanding and enjoyment of Lucretius' poetry and how negligent our scholars have been about it. Lucretius has been arguing for the indestructibility of matter. Rain, for example, perishes when it goes into the ground but it is not destroyed, it reappears as the moisture in all living things:

postremo pereunt imbres, ubi eos pater aether
in gremium matris terrai praecipitauit;
at nitidae surgunt fruges, ramique uirescunt
arboribus, crescunt ipsae fetuque grauantur.
hinc alitur porro nostrum genus atque ferarum,
hinc laetas urbes pueris florere uidemus
frondiferasque nouis auibus canere undique siluas,
hinc fessae pecudes pingui per pabula laeta
corpora deponunt et candens lacteus umor
uberibus manat distentis, hinc noua proles
artubus infirmis teneras lasciua per herbas
ludit lacte mero mentes perculsa nouellas.
  haud igitur penitus pereunt quaecumque uidentur,
quando alit ex alio reficit natura nec ullam
rem gigni patitur, nisi morte adiuta aliena.
  1 250-64

Lastly the rains cease to exist when the sky, the father of all things hurls them into the lap of mother earth. But the shining crops arise and the branches grow green upon the trees, the trees themselves grow and are heavy with fruit; from this in turn the human race and the animals are nourished. It is this moisture which makes our thriving cities flower with children, and sets the woods now in leaf singing all about us with new birds. This is the richness which wearies the flocks as they lay down their bodies in the rich grass, and the milky-white juice oozes from their swollen udders. This is what assaults the senses of the new generation shaky on their legs, frisking on the delicate grass, innocents drunk with neat milk.

So nothing that you see wholly perishes, since nature renews one thing from another and allows nothing to come to life without help from the death of something else.

This extract begins with a rationalized statement of the ancient idea of the divine marriage between sky and earth, which has caught the imagination of so many poets. The typically Lucretian detail here is *praecipitauit*, which conveys the violence of the insemination. Typically this is toned down in Virgil's imitation:

uere tument terrae et genitalia semina poscunt.

tum pater omnipotens fecundis imbribus aether
coniugis in gremium laetae descendit

Georgics II 324-6

Ronsard, on the other hand, in his *L'Avant-venue du printemps* goes back to *praecipitauit:*

Ja le ciel d'amour s'enflame
et dans le sein de sa fame
ja se rue en s'élançant.

Despite this, Fraisse surprisingly suggests that Ronsard was here influenced by Virgil and not by Lucretius. Klepl too fails to do justice to the image of maternity which runs through this whole passage.

After copulation, parturition. 'The trees themselves grow and are heavy with fruit' – *fetuque grauantur* clearly refers to pregnancy, but our translations obscure it. In line 255 'We see our thriving cities flowering with children'. *Laeta*, joyful, fertile, is also an ambivalent term, and Lucretius here, and Virgil in the passage just quoted, exploit the ambivalence. In Virgil the earth is *laeta*, fertile, she is also *laeta coniunx*, a wife delighted by the attentions of her husband, like the ewe and the heifer in Ovid *Ars Amatoria* 2 485. Bailey and Latham throw away *florere*, offering 'alive with children', and 'blest with children'. This substitution of cliché for Latin metaphor ruins the logic as well as the poetry. Here, after the careful distinction of three

types of tree growth – the foliage, the over-all size, the
fruiting – when Lucretius says that we see the fertile cities
flowering with children, he is surely throwing out a suggestion about the growth of cities. As flower and fruit are
to the tree, so children are to the city. And he is hinting at
the unity of all things, as he does so profoundly around 2 76
inter se mortales mutua uiuunt. Again, in line 256, when the
woods sing all about us with new birds, it will come as no
surprise to learn that Bailey has 'leafy woods ringing with
young birds' cry' and Latham has 'every leafy thicket loud
with new broods of songsters'. Neither 'ringing' nor 'loud'
has the precision, simplicity or daring of the original *canere.*
Nor is *frondiferas* in this line a vacuous ornamental epithet.
The juxtaposition of *frondiferas nouis* reminds us that the
foliage too is new and has arrived just before the nestlings.
The 'leafy woods' of English translators miss this nuance,
although nuance by juxtaposition is a vital resource of
Latin poetic style.

After parturition, lactation, as also in 5 811-25. 'This is
what fattens the flocks till they let themselves wearily down
in the lush pastures and the milky white moisture oozes
from their distended udders'. The milky abundance of this
description shows the poet's gluttonous enjoyment of the
world about him, and is strictly in the argument. He is
claiming that the rain which was hurled upon the earth is
not destroyed, but regroups to form an abundance of vital
moisture.

After feeding, play. Amongst the pictures in line 260, we
see in *artubus infirmis* the frail trembling legs of kids and
foals and calves and lambs; the juxtaposition *infirmis
teneras* suggests that nature has provided a soft carpet for
these rickety legs; *lasciua* hints at the sexuality of their
play. In 261 we have the astounding explanation of their
behaviour. *Merum*, unmixed, is almost always used of wine,
and to drink wine unmixed, as these young creatures had

done, is asking for trouble. *Perculsus* is used of an extremely violent impact or assault. They have been drinking *neat* milk, and it has knocked them sideways. The juxtaposition *perculsa nouellas* suggests it's the first time out for these young things. All this is in the Latin, but I see very little of it in Bailey's 'their baby hearts thrilling with the pure milk'.

The importance of the literal sense of words in Lucretius can be confirmed by a consideration of his use of *fulgur*, the lightning flash. In 122 B C Etna had erupted and destroyed the town of Catana, and Lucretius was sure that it would erupt again:

> . . . hic Aetnaea minantur
> murmura flammarum rursum se colligere iras
> faucibus e ruptos iterum uis ut uomat ignis
> ad caelumque ferat flammai fulgura rursum.
>
> 1 722-5

When he prophesies that it will spew the broken fires from its throat once again, and will again hurl the lightnings of its flame up to the sky, this is no tautology. 'The electrical phenomena attending on an eruption are often of great intensity and splendour. The dark ash-laden clouds of vapour are shot through and through by volcanic lightning sometimes in rapid horizontal flashes then in oblique forked streaks, or again in tortuous lines compared to fiery serpents, whilst the borders of the cloud may be brilliant with electrical scintillations.'[3] In Einarsson's booklet on the eruption of Surtsey, one of the pictures shows a single lightning flash rising straight up out of the cone of the volcano, and a plate in 'L'Italia Fisica' in the series *Conosci L'Italia*, published by the Touring Club Italiano, shows such flashes emerging from Vesuvius. Line 725 therefore is a precise and vivid description, and is differentiated from line 724, and the literal force of *flammai fulgura* is necessary to the sense and poetry of the passage.

Against this literal translation it may be urged that the dictionaries offer four passages in classical Latin where *fulgur* refers not to lightning but only to brightness. These are all in Lucretius.

In 2 164 he is attempting to describe the velocity of the movement of atoms by comparing it with the speed of sunlight. Although this is wonderfully fast, sunlight has to push its way past many obstacles, whereas an atom moving through the void can meet no obstacle, and therefore *a fortiori* its movement is very much faster, 'it traverses an extent of space very much greater in the time it takes for the lightnings of the sun to spread over the sky',

multiplexque loci spatium transcurrere eodem
tempore quo solis peruulgant fulgura caelum.

2 163-4

When Lucretius talks of the lightnings of the sun, this is not simply 'a fine variant', in Bailey's phrase. It is typical of Lucretius' poetic genius suddenly to give an extra thrust to the knife of his argument by this sudden appeal to what we have all seen with our own eyes. 'The atoms are faster than sunlight, and that is as fast as a flash of lightning.' The dictionaries are wrong in taking the lightning out of this passage. The same mistake occurs in a very similar argu-ment in 4 190.

In 6 182, in the description of the different causes of lightning, the hot wind whirling around in a black cloud emits seeds of heat which make the winking lightnings of flame,

semina quae faciunt nictantia fulgura flammae.

Here again the dictionaries cannot be right in suggesting that *fulgura* does not mean lightning flashes, any more than the translators can be right in rendering *nictantia* as 'pulsing', 'flickering', 'zig-zag'. In this phrase Lucretius suggests that a lightning flash is as fast as the blinking of an eye, and so produces poetry by associating the powerful with the insignificant, the immense with the minute, the theoretic with the empiric, the cosmic with the personal, and all this juggling goes to ground in the translations quoted.

In 5 296 Lucretius is explaining that light is not con-tinuous, but is a succession of separate light images so rapid that our eyes apprehend them as continuous. After explain-ing sunlight in these terms he turns to earthly lights, to hanging lamps and to torches 'bright with flashing light-nings and rich with the thick darkness of their smoke. These too, like the sun, hasten to keep up the supply of new light with the aid of their flame, they are swift to tremble with their fires, they are swift . . .'

. . . pendentes lychni claraeque coruscis
fulguribus pingues multa e caligine taedae
consimili properant ratione, ardore ministro,
subpeditare nouom lumen, tremere ignibus instant,
instant . . .
    5 295 - 9

In his insistence upon the speed of these successions of flame, Lucretius talks of torches with their flashing light-nings in order to vivify his argument by reminding us of what we have all seen with our own eyes – the speed of the lightning flash. So if we remove the lightning from *coruscis fulguribus* we impoverish the poetry and mortify the argument.

Therefore in all these five passages *fulgur* refers to light-ning, as it always does in classical Latin, and the poetry cannot be understood if the literal sense of the word is not apprehended.

'Imaging is, in itself', according to Dryden, 'the very height and life of poetry.' This is true of the poetry of Lucretius. Yet his images are frequently not explained by commentators and not respected by translators. Even those writing expressly on his imagery have done little more than pass general judgments supported by lists of paraphrased

examples. Popular though it is among writers on classical
literature, paraphrase kills poetry, and in Lucretius (where
so much depends upon the acuity of the detail), it mutilates
the corpse. This book will attempt throughout to elucidate
neglected images in the hope of increasing our appreciation
of the height and life of the poetry. This should have been
done long ago. In 1931 Davies was demanding it in his
attack upon 'our pernicious insensibility'. 'Lucretius' use of
Metaphor is unique in European Literature yet almost
imperceptible to modern taste. And there is only one
method of perceiving it; a scrupulous reconstruction of the
atmosphere of all metaphorical words.' He ends this famous
article: 'Research into the imagery of ancient poets, however scientifically conducted, is not an end in itself; the
metaphors of Lucretius, however ingenious, must not be
mere ingenuities; they must be quickened into poetry by a
sense of the magnificent "earnestness of the man", an
earnestness so forceful and sincere that it seems to impose
on us almost as a moral obligation the elucidation of his
fullest meaning.'

Davies' work has often been cited with approval, but
never been acted upon.

2. Characteristics of the Images

'He had that acute and sharp sensuous awareness essential to all great poets. He was physically aware of textures, surfaces, colours, patterns of every kind; acutely aware of earth's diurnal course, of growth and decay, of animality in man and vitality in all things.' Herbert Read.

This chapter will give a brief survey of some features of Lucretius' imagery, the nicety of their detail, their function in the argument, their plenitude.

¶ *Nicety of Detail.* The minute details of Lucretius' images are the first to suffer from imprecise treatment. Minute descriptions of observed phenomena are the proper business of the scientist rather than the poet, but such descriptions may sometimes be a part of poetry, as when, for example, they draw our attention to some detail which is not obvious or which is particularly significant or evocative. When we read

with sixteen stamens equidistant set

this may be good botany. But when Lucretius says that birds flying around Lake Avernus are overcome by sulphurous vapours and fall to the ground *molli ceruice profusae* (6 744), *profusae* suggests that the bodies of the birds lose their living tension in mid air and fall forward inertly along the line of their flight, and *molli ceruice* suggests that the neck which has been out-stretched in flight is now slack in the death fall. Pity the poor translator at a phrase like this, but he ought to be able to do something better than 'with soft necks outstretched'.

Sometimes it is the suggestiveness of the detail which charges the passage with poetry. In 4 220, for example, he refers to the spray from sea waves as the gnawer-away of walls around the shore, *exesor moerorum litora circum*. This reminds us that sand-stone walls near the sea do come to look as though creatures had gnawed away at them. So again in the sixth book where he is explaining that the sea suffers great loss of moisture through evaporation by the sun's heat:

... uidemus enim uestis umore madentis
exsiccare suis radiis ardentibus solem;
at pelage multa et late substrata uidemus.

   6 617-619

For we see that dripping clothes are completely dried out by the burning rays of the sun; and yet we see many oceans spread out far and wide beneath it.

Here the oceans are sheets laid out on a drying green (cf. 1 306) and *substrata* is the life of the poetry. The trans-lators with their 'stretching wide beneath' make a small but fatal change. Again, we can all imagine what an earthquake would be like, but Lucretius fastens upon the fact that the tops of the buildings would sway more than the middle, the middle more than the bottom, the bottom very little,

   summa magis mediis, media imis, ima perhilum.   6 576

This is not the most sublime line in the whole corpus of Latin poetry, but it does exemplify Lucretius' ability to select the telling and illuminating detail, an ability he shares with other great poets; and with children. Thiel puts his finger on it. 'As a boy I had observed what Lucretius described, but now I have got out of the way of noticing it.' In a book devoted partly to the poetry of Lucretius, it would be absurd to pass this line without talking about the sound of it. Some facts about the sounds are that the letter *m* occurs eight times, that in the tremors of the first half of the line the word accent (′) does not coincide with the verse ictus (°), *mágis médiis média* whereas in the stability at the end of the line they do coincide, *ímis íma perhílum*, and each of these coincidences is upon a long *i*. At such moments

English commentators on Latin verse usually collapse in a paroxysm of metaphor, the repeated *m* evoking the move-ment menacing the massive structure, the heterodyne bodying forth the dislocation of the upper storeys and the homodyne on the long *i* providing in audible verity the pedal point on which the whole fugal edifice finds its final stability and consummation. It would be better to set against such passages a sign meaning 'read this aloud'. But there is no need for a diacritical sign in Lucretius. Every line should be read aloud and listened to. The relationship between sound and sense is so multiple, so complex, so swift and subtle, that discussion can never catch it and would kill it if it did.

A last example of the importance of the minute detail in this imagery will be the passage in the fifth book where Lucretius includes spontaneous movement as one of the possible explanations of the motions of the stars:

>   . . . siue ipsi serpere possunt,
> quo cuiusque cibus uocat atque inuitat euntis,
> flammea per caelum pascentis corpora passim.
>   5 523-5

. . . or whether they can each creep about unaided wherever their food calls them and invites them as they go feeding their fiery bodies throughout the sky.

Each star is going its own way wandering about in search of its own particular food. Being stars their bodies are fiery, and so, on this theory, is their food. Translators shy away from creeping or crawling stars. They move, they glide, they even swim, ils puissent glisser, können sie glissen. Bailey alone of my group makes them creep but doesn't see why:

> nam saepe in colli tondentes pabula laeta
> lanigerae *reptant* pecudes quo *quamque uocantes*
> *inuitant* herbae gemmantes rore recenti.
>   2 317-9

*For often the flocks of woolly sheep cropping the rich pasture
on a hillside creep about wherever each is called and invited
by the grass jewelled with fresh dew.*

Even sheep don't crawl, *reptare*, but Lucretius makes them
do so here because he is in this context taking a distant
view. The detail here is fascinating because he has caught
the slowness of the movement (*reptant*) which suggests a
legless progress across the face of the hill, the independent
course of each sheep (*quamque*), the different blandish-
ments to which each responds (*uocantes inuitant*). All of
these perceptive and telling details are used again of the
feeding of stars, (*serpere, cuiusque, uocat atque inuitat*). The
man who likes sheep, or watches them, will be able to
expound the agricultural passage and the luminous three
lines that follow it, but when he comes to the astronomy
he can only remain speechless before the audacity of poetic
genius.

It is easy to fall into a way of talking about the precise
observation and vivid descriptive powers of Lucretius. But
such terms beg a question. They imply that Lucretius had
watched women dyeing clothes, and sat at a fire burning
bits of wool or studied sheep grazing on a distant hill
(6 1074-7, 4 376, 2 317-22). There is no evidence for this.
So many of these are the stock illustrations from Hellenistic
philosophy, and so many others must have been culled
from philosophical writings which have not survived, that
we have no right to treat anything in this poem as auto-
biographical information.

Townend, in Dudley (103-5), is tempted to believe
Lucretius when he uses first person verbs like *uidi* and
quaerimus, and yet he admits that the motes in the sunbeam
which provide him with one of his examples of such verbs
had already been used by Democritus and Aristotle. In fact
of the five examples of stock philosophical arguments
which he cites on page 103, three contain such verbs

(*cernimus* 4 353, *uehimur* 4 387, *demersimus* 6 149). The truth stares us in the face. Lucretius is steeped in Greek philosophy. He is also a keen visualizer and a brilliant teacher, and knows that a claim to autopsy lends immediacy to the drabbest exposition. We cannot therefore tell whether he had these experiences himself, or read about them, or both. Did Lucretius ever hear seven fold echoes as he claims in 4 577? Did he ever put a magnet under a pot of iron filings and watch them seething (6 1044)? Did he ever actually experience the conversion experience of 3 14-30 with all the features studied in William James' *Varieties of Religious Experience*, the holy books, the voice, the terror, the vision of infinity, the immanence of the deity, the home of the gods, the light, the peace, the joy, the horror? It is fatuous to expect any answer to such questions. When I talk of Lucretius' experience, or observation or descriptions, I do so to avoid cumbrous circumlocutions. Whether he is writing from his own experience of life, or from his books, or both, we cannot know.

¶ *Dialectical Function.* In Dudley (51), in an eloquent evocation of the range of phenomena described by Lucretius one of the first examples given by Wormell to illustrate 'the poet's acute sensory awareness of his environment' is 'the gradual wearing away of the ring', in 1 312, *anulus in digito subter tenuatur habendo*. But the ring is not quite worn away; it is made thinner by wearing, and the acute word is *subter*, on the under side. It is the precision of this which gives the reader some sort of poetic experience by setting his visual and tactile imagination to work.

But this is not pure titillation of the senses. *Subter* is necessary to the argument because he is talking about attrition and *subter* focuses our eyes upon the point of friction. Again and again the images in Lucretius, down to the smallest detail, are functional, and their function is to clarify and enforce the argument of the poem. After making glowing claims for his poetry at the beginning of the fourth book, Lucretius drags them all down to the ground by his prosaic statement that the charm of poetry seems not to be wholly pointless:

... musaeo contingens cuncta lepore.
id quoque enim non ab nulla ratione uidetur.
    4 9-10

The *ratio* of his poetry is that it sweetens the seemingly bitter but life-giving draught of Epicureanism. And the *ratio* of these images is the rigorous logical work they are set to do in their contexts. This is one of the things which gives such drastic intensity to the poetry of Lucretius, and again it is a quality often lost in paraphrases.

A decisive example occurs when Lucretius refers to his belief that the earth is capable of spontaneous generation of worms:

        ... uermisque efferuere, terram
intempestiuos quom putor cepit ob imbris
    2 928-9

... worms seethe when putrefaction comes over the earth as a result of excessive rains.

We know from 5 798-806 that this terrestrial generation required heat as well as moisture. *Efferuere* then is a quick reference to that. The earth is boiling over with worms. It is a breach of science when the translators choose to swarm out, entwimmeln, sortir en grouillant, burst forth and teem.

To take another example, in arguing that the invisible atoms are capable of the groupings which constitute our visible world, he refers to the diversity of the animal kingdom, sheep horses cattle, and then of the constituent parts, their bones blood veins heat moisture entrails nerves, all of them constituted by different arrangements of atoms. Then he goes on to argue that anything that burns has within it, amongst other things, matter which can produce fire:

tum porro quae cumque igni flammata cremantur,
si nihil praeterea, tamen haec in corpore condunt,
unde ignem iacere et lumen submittere possint
scintillasque agere ac late differre fauillam.

2 672-5

Then further whatever flames and burns with fire conceals within its body if nothing else, at least the matter which enables it to shoot out fire, to throw up light, to drive out sparks and spread ash all round.

This keen sense of these four material products of fire is again poetic for its enlargement of our sensory experience, and again germane to the argument, the diversity of all matter. Animals have different substances in their bodies and each of these substances is complex. So what is combustible has fire within it amongst other things, and that fire is in itself at least four separate substances.

Lucretius is expounding a materialist philosophy which explains the whole of our world and of our experience in terms of the movements of invisible material particles. So again and again he has to infer the behaviour of these particles from the behaviour of visible phenomena, rivers, wind and sea, fire, light and all the rest. To take a more domestic example, from the fact that liquids can be scooped or spilt as easily as poppy seed, he deduces in 2 451-5 that their constituent atoms are round and smooth like individual poppy seeds. The philosophical subject matter of this poem is not an impediment to the poetry, it is rather the stimulus for the impassioned observation and contentious contemplation of the material world which contribute so much to the poetic intensity of the work. This book is an attempt to challenge the vulgar error that the *De Rerum Natura* consists of oases of poetry in deserts of philosophy; to challenge those like Fitton Brown who find that 'vast

3

portions of the poem are sorry stuff from the poet's point of view'; to challenge the influential dogmatism of Mommsen, 'it is a remarkable fatality that this man of extraordinary talents, far superior in originality of poetic endowments to most if not all his contemporaries . . . made the most singular mistake in the selection of a subject. . . . The task of poetically unfolding this mechanical view of the world was of such a nature that never probably did poet expend life and art on a more ungrateful theme.' If Mommsen is right in claiming that Lucretius is 'one of the most brilliant stars in the poorly illuminated expanse of Roman literature', many of the passages cited in this book, chosen without any fear of 'the dreariness of physical demonstrations', will show that the mechanism of our world is a fit subject for poetry, and that Lucretius is a fit poet for it. Bardon puts it with Gallic elegance, 'Chez Lucrèce la métaphore est poésie parce qu'elle est évidence'.

¶ *Plenitude.* Perhaps the most striking characteristic of Lucretius' imagery is its opulence. If you press the lower part of your eye you see double. Lucretius doesn't leave it at that, but gives four particular examples of what would be most conspicuous if you made this experiment indoors:

> bina lucernarum florentia lumina flammis,
> binaque per totas aedis geminare supellex,
> et duplicis hominum facies et corpora bina.
>   4 450-2

double lamp-lights flowering with flame, all the furniture in the house seen double, men with two faces and double bodies.

Again in the same book, in arguing against a teleological view of anatomy, that our bodies were made in order to fulfil their functions, that our eyes were made to see:

. . . et ut proferre queamus	825
proceros passus, ideo fastigia posse	827
surarum ac feminum pedibus fundata plicari	826

. . . and that the top of our calves and of our thighs, based
upon the feet are able to be bent on purpose that we should
be able to take long strides forward . . .

Here the syntax is crammed and distorted. He means that
we have joints at the top of our thighs and also our
calves, and that the bottom of the calves is based upon
the feet. This is not however obscurity or incompetence.
This telescoping of the logic vividly conveys the articulation
of the leg bones, and this in turn is vividly relevant to the
main argument, his rebuttal of the Watchmaker Fallacy.
The complexity of the phenomenon does not prove that it
had a Creator.

Meteorological, domestic, rural, technological, theatrical,
sexual – there was no limit to his observations. They
range from the unimaginably minute to the infinitely
vast:

primum animalia sunt iam partim tantula, corum
tertia pars nulla possit ratione uideri.
horum intestinum quoduis quale esse putandumst?
quid cordis globus aut oculi?

4 116-9

First of all there are some animals so small that if you
divided them into three the parts would not be visible. What
sort of thing do you think one of their intestines would be
like? And what about their round heart or their eyes?

He goes on to ask about the size of the atoms which constitute the soul of such an animalcule. So too, in 3 381-90 a
speck of chalk, strands of cobweb and gossamer, or the
flea's foot, touch our skin unnoticed because they touch
a space between soul particles. The infinitely vast is the stuff
of the poetry at the end of the second book, so keenly
appreciated by Klingner, and also around 1 1002-5 where
the extent of space is said to be so large that if a lightning
flash traversed it for endless time, the distance remaining
to be traversed would be not a whit the less.

Thiel has referred to the childish clarity of Lucretius'
visualization. The infantile sometimes verges on the lunatic,
and the sanity of Lucretius has been called into question by
Postgate, citing the history of primitive man with which he
ends the fifth book. Throughout this passage Lucretius'
powers of visualization give immediacy to the writing,
nowhere more than in the description of the confusion
which resulted when animals were trained for use in warfare, elephants, bulls, lions, boars, savaging friend as well
as foe. Having reached this point in his imaginative reconstruction of prehistory, Lucretius realizes that it is not
wholly credible that people should willingly have used a
suicidal weapon, but it is too much to require a poet to
expunge this great picture of trained animals boiling up in
the heat of action in the middle of the wounding and shouting and fleeing and terror and tumult:

si quos ante domi domitos satis esse putabant,
efferuescere cernebant in rebus agundis
uolneribus clamore fuga terrore tumultu
    5 1334-6

So Lucretius saves his fantasy by suggesting two possible
explanations, one, that this may not in fact have happened
in our world, but in one of the infinite number of worlds in
the universe slightly different from ours; two, that those
who took these uncontrollable animals into battle did so as
a counsel of despair because they were hopelessly out-
numbered or without arms and were determined not to
perish without hurting their enemies. This *reductio ad
extremum* of visualization, vindicated by elaborate logic,
seemed to Postgate to be the work of an imbecile, but
readers of Lucretius will be accustomed to living with
extremes, and will not find them inconsistent with sanity.
For example they are told, in the resounding hieratic
language which Lucretius so often affects when he touches
upon superstitions, that nothing burns with a more crack-

ling flame, with a more awful noise than the laurel of Delphic Apollo:

nec res ulla magis quam Phoebi Delphica laurus
terribili sonitu flamma crepitante crematur.

6 154-5

They will even enjoy the assertion that there are so many thousands of snake-handed elephants in India that the country is fortified by an ivory palisade (2 537-8). 'Palisade' is Rouse's translation. The tusks of the elephants are the slats of the stockade. The walls and Walle, and ramparts and remparts and bulwarks of other translators are non-sense. But no doubt they were behind the old notion that the 'ivory tower' is etymologically connected with this passage.

This chapter has had two main purposes: to protest against the treachery of paraphrase and mistranslation, and in so doing to isolate three characteristics of Lucretius' imagery. This is an arbitrary analysis in that so many of his images exhibit these and other characteristics in varying degrees. These however are perhaps worth attempting to pick out because they convey a good impression of the tone of his poetry, and because from now on in this book we shall be able to take them for granted. The detail, the logical usefulness and the abundance of Lucretius' imagery, we shall either pass by in silence or refer to as something which we do not need to establish by argument. In tackling this huge subject from now on I shall divide his images according to their subject matter, in an attempt to gather an impression of how he uses them. The subjects chosen are the theatre, the circus, building, fire and light. These are only samples, and they do not include some very important topics, natural phenomena for example, and warfare, which is well discussed by Rozelaar. My subjects have been chosen not because of their frequency or importance, but mainly in order to break new ground and gradually to gather at the end of each chapter some general impression of how Lucretius uses his imagery.

But first, in the third chapter, I shall turn aside to look at Lucretius' place in the traditions of ancient poetry and to answer a charge which has recently been levelled against some of his images.

3. Lucretius and Epic

¶ *Conventional Epic Periphrases.* In the recent book of essays collected by Dudley, three writers discuss the imagery of Lucretius (51-2, 60-1, 86-91, 95-114), and each of these writers cites Davies' article. But none of them has taken his most fundamental point, on which I ended my first chapter, that the images of Lucretius are not yet fully understood.

For instance, on page 99 Townend accords 'some weight to criticism of those metaphors which Lucretius found ready made in earlier writers', and in particular to the conventional epic periphrases, *liquoris uitigeni laticem* and *flos Bacchi* for wine, *flos flammai* for fire, and *caeli cauernas*, the caverns of the sky. This chapter is an attempt to shed light upon these epic periphrases and in particular to defend them against this criticism.

Townend argues that *flos Bacchi* in 3 221, the flower of Bacchus, is an epic periphrasis which does not seem to assist the feeling of the passage, although here *flos* appears to have the sense of 'bouquet'. It would indeed be monstrous to object to *flos* in this context since Lucretius is arguing precisely, falsely too but that does not matter, that when perfume loses its fragrance and when wine goes flat, there is no loss of mass or weight. The *bouquet* of the wine *is* what he is talking about. What is he to call it if not by its proper Latin name? To object to Bacchus being used as a synonym for wine would also be unfair. This trick with gods' names is very frequent in Latin poetry (cf. Williams on Virgil *Aeneid* 5 77 and add the dissertation by Gross), and

Lucretius has already explained his sceptical attitude to
it in 2 655 - 60.

The flower of flame which flashes at 1 900 is said by
Townend to be 'a rather dubious Homeric metaphor' because
it occurs not in the text of Homer but in Plutarch's citation
of it in *Moralia* 934B. But far nearer home than Homer is
the occurrence of this metaphor in early Latin poetry,
Uolcani opera haec flammis fieri flora (Naevius *tragicorum
fragmenta* 48 R), and in the conjecture *florebant flammis*
(Ennius *Annales* 323 V). More important than this is the
context. Lucretius is here denying that every substance
has within it particles of every other substance. His imaginary opponent invokes forest fires caused by branches rubbing
together. Lucretius in reply insists that these are not the
agglomeration of particles of fire, but of particles of indeter-
minate matter, of atoms, which cause fire; not particles of
fire, but seeds of fire:

    'at saepe in magnis fit montibus' inquis 'ut altis
    arboribus uicina cacumina summa terantur
    inter se ualidis facere id cogentibus austris,
    donec flammai fulserunt flore coorto'.   900
    scilicet et non est lignis tamen insitus ignis,
    uerum semina sunt ardoris multa, terendo
    quae cum confluxere, creant incendia siluis.
      1 897- 903

*'But' you say 'it often happens in great mountains that the
topmost branches of tall trees which are close together are
made to rub on each other by powerful winds until they flash
out with the gathered flower of flame.'*
*That's true enough, but for all that the fire is not grafted into
the wood, rather there are many seeds of heat which flow
together as a result of the rubbing and generate a blaze
among the woods.*

In the first place *flos flammai* is not put forward as Lucretius'
own phrase but is attributed by him to an imaginary

antagonist. This observation will be developed later in this chapter. In the second place Lucretius picks this up in *insitus*, *semina* and *creant*, and plays with it with an acute awareness of the force of the metaphor, and a devastating application of it to the argument in hand. The fire in branches is not an alien stock grafted on to the wood, *insita*, it is not particles of fire; it is rather particles which can cause fire, *semina ardoris*. There are no grounds for adverse criticism of this image.

Townend equally accepts such criticism against *caeli cauernas*, the caverns of the sky, in 4 171 and in 6 252. This last example is a towering demonstration of the grandeur of the imagination of Lucretius. Throughout this passage he is thinking of the clouds as great edifices piled above our heads, as we see from *nubibus extructis* 247, 268 and

. . . nisi inaedificata superne
multa forent multis exempto nubila sole
  6 264 - 5

where 'cloud built up on cloud depriving us of the sun' may well be a swift play with a matter which must have caused much concern and some lawsuits to people who lived in an expanding tenement city like Rome (cf. *luminum*, Cicero *de Oratore* 1 173).

But the force of this image is even more complex. In both the passages from which it is cited the immediate context is the same:

. . . uti tenebras omnis Acherunta rearis
liquisse et magnas caeli complesse cauernas
  4 170 -1 (6 251 - 2)

(*The sky is so dark*) *that you would think that all the darkness had left the Underworld and filled the great caverns of the sky.*

Acheron, the Underworld, is honeycombed with caverns (6 536 - 542). The suggestion is that the darkness has moved from one cavernous habitat to another. Each of these nuances must have flicked the mind of the reader who was attuned to the style of this poet and familiar with his thinking, each in less time than it takes to write a word. The critic is pedestrian in pursuit but at least he can show that before we pass pejorative judgments upon these images, we should study them respectfully in their whole context. We should also know a great deal, which at the moment we do not know, about Lucretius' language. It is highly signifi-cant that the images discussed in this chapter all occur in early Roman poetry: *flos flammai* we have seen above, *flos Liberi* and *cauernas caeli* as in the passages cited in Munro's commentary and in Ennius *Scaenica* 112 V *caua caeli*.

This leaves 'the juice of the vine-born liquid' in 5 14, in a passage full of resounding poetic periphrases. Lucretius has often suffered because commentators have failed to notice his trick of putting words on the lips of his opponents. Being merciless and often unfair in controversy, he regularly mimics their style of speech. A clear but benign example occurs in the imitation of Ennius in 3 1025-35. More indirect and malicious is his mockery of Heracleitus and his supporters in

> ueraque constituunt quae belle tangere possunt
> auris et lepido quae sunt fucata sonore.

  1 643-4

They take as truth what can tickle their ears pleasantly, what is dyed in an attractive sound.

Here the adoration of the Heracleiteans is suggested in the adverb *belle* and the adjective *lepidus*, which Lucretius never uses anywhere else. The potential malice of these words is well brought out by Catullus 78 which was too scabrous to print in the recent Oxford edition of this poet. The triple synaesthesia in the Lucretius, tactile, visual and aural, suggests the specious tortuosities of Heracleitus' style.

Equally malicious is his mockery of oracular language:

qua prius adgrediar quam de re fundere fata
sanctius et multo certa ratione magis quam
Pythia quae tripode a Phoebi lauroque profatur,
multa tibi expediam doctis solacia dictis.

5 110-3

Before I set myself to pour forth my oracles on this subject
more binding and much more certain than those uttered by
the Pythian priestess from the tripod and laurel of Apollo,
I shall unfold many wise words of comfort for you.

More important is his mimicry in 6 852 where he is discussing the miraculous spring in the shrine of Hammon
which was said to be cold during the day and warm at
night:

hunc homines fontem nimis admirantur et acri
sole putant subter terras feruescere partim,
nox ubi terribili terras caligine texit.
quod nimis a uerast longe ratione remotum.

6 850-3

Men are too inclined to marvel at this spring, and some
believe that it is heated by the scorching sun beneath the earth
when night veils the earth with terrifying darkness. But this
is far removed from the truth.

This is important because Anderson has argued that night
is a symbol in Lucretius, referred to unemotionally at the
beginning of the poem as being neither a good thing nor a
bad, but by the time Lucretius had reached his last book,
he had become more pessimistic, and contrary to his
conscious philosophy, he gave way here to this momentary
fear which he had previously rejected. All this is far removed from the truth, because night is not a symbol in
Lucretius, any more than war, death or the sea, which
Anderson also cites in developing his case, and because
this superstitious fear of darkness is here attributed by
Lucretius to the credulous people who thought that the sun

could heat the bottom of a spring more effectively during
the night than the surface of it during the day. The assonance in *terribili terras* guides the tone of the reading voice.
So, then, with the 'juice of the vine-born liquid' in the preface to the fifth book, we have a priestly utterance, with
uitigeni a parody of the cult titles so dear to the *uates* whom
Lucretius detested:

  namque Ceres *fertur* fruges Liberque liquoris
  uitigeni laticem mortalibus instituisse.
  5 14-15
*For Demeter and Bacchus are said to have ordained grain
crops for mortals and the juice of the vine-born fluid.*

This is surely the explanation of the other poetic periphrases
in this whole passage, where Lucretius is belittling the
achievements of Hercules in order to magnify by contrast
the achievements of Epicurus. The famous great maw of
the Nemean lion, the hydra palisaded by its venomous
snakes, the triple-chested violence of triple Geryon are all
stuffed dummies, heavily padded with epic fustian. They
are all harmless to us, and would be harmless even if
Hercules had never dealt with them, whereas the human
evils that Epicurus overcame on our behalf are still be-
setting us. When Townend writes, 'the periphrasis for
uinum quoted above does not seem to assist the feeling of
the passage', he is failing to notice this use of parody in
argument which is so characteristic of this brutal and
unscrupulous controversialist. It is a weapon which has
rebounded on Lucretius elsewhere, nowhere with more
deadly results than at the end of Book 3, where he writes his
great dialogue with the man who is afraid to die. Again and
again the arguments of his antagonist are brought forward
by writers on Lucretius as Lucretius' own deepest, most
irrepressible sentiments:

  '. . . misero misere' aiunt 'omnia ademit
  una dies . . .'

'at nos horrifico cinefactum te prope busto
insatiabiliter defleuimus, aeternumque
nulla dies nobis maerorem e pectore demet.'

3 898-9, 906-8

Instead of taking such statements as manifestations of
L'Anti-Lucrèce chez Lucrèce, we should remember that
each of these arguments is punctually and brusquely
rejected by Lucretius speaking in his own voice, and later
even more peremptorily by Nature, who takes over his part
in the dialogue. Surely these pathetic rhetorical figures and
astonishing rhythms are meant as sarcastic caricatures of the
mawkish clichés used by such *stulti* and *baratri*. *Insatiabiliter*
for instance is not necessarily an elevated word. Its only
other use in Lucretius is of swine rolling in filth, 6 978.

Such periphrases are in the Epic style, but in using them
Lucretius is putting the Epic style to vigorous and effective
use. It might be worthwhile to look at the ornamental
epithets in Lucretius in this connection. For instance
Palmer refers to 'the use of the constant ornamental epithet
in 1 250-64'. Ornamental yes, but the discussion of this
passage in my first chapter showed that none of them is
otiose. Every single epithet is working wonders in its
context at a logical, or emotional, or sensuous level. To take
only a few other examples from the first book: *uiuida tellus*
178, the earth is alive 'quickened' in Munro's translation
because she is the mother who has received the *semina
rerum*, and is bringing forth her tender young to the boundaries of light; in *fluctifrago suspensae in litore* 305, the
shore is wave-breaking, because Lucretius is talking about
clothes which have been hung up to dry and are saturated
by spray; in *rigidum permanat frigus ad ossa*, 355, the *rigid*
cold oozing through to the bone, makes a penetrating
paradox with its suggestions of steel and ice, a conceit later
developed by Martial writing about the slave boy who was
killed by a falling icicle:

tabuit in calido uulnere mucro tener
    4 18 6
its brittle sword-point melted in the warm wound.
¶ *Ennius and Homer.* There is no reason to hold it against
Lucretius that he imitated Homer and Ennius. The quality
of his imitations should save him from that. Consider first
his adaptation of an image in Ennius, and then his translation of a passage in Homer:
    homo qui erranti comiter mostrat uiam,
    quasi lumen de suo lumine accendat, facit:
    nihilo minus ipsi lucet, cum illi accenderit.

Ennius *Scaenica*, 398-400v
*If you obligingly point out the way to somebody who is lost,
you are so to speak lighting his torch from your own, and
your own torch gives no less light after lighting his.*
    haec sic pernosces parua perductus opella;
    namque alid ex alio clarescet, nec tibi caeca
    nox iter eripiet, quin ultima naturai
    peruideas: ita res accendent lumina rebus.

Lucretius 1 1114-7
*So you will comprehend all this fully, being led to the end
by making a little effort: one thing will become clear from
another and night will not take away your view of the road
and prevent you from seeing in full the ultimate truths of
nature. So will one thing light a torch for the next.*
In Ennius one man lights another's torch from his own and his
civility costs him nothing; in Lucretius, Epicureanism is a series
of doctrines in the dark, but as each one is illumined it trans-
mits light forward. The basic image is the kindling of one light
from another, but each poet employs it for a wholly different
purpose, and Lucretius is no more a mindless imitator than
is Dante:
    Facesti come quei che va di notte
    che porta il lume dietro e sé non giova
    ma dopo sé fa le persone dotte.

The same poetic independence is noted by Giancotti in his study of Lucretius' most famous adaptation of Homer:

ἡ μὲν ἄρ' ὣς εἰποῦσ' ἀπέβη γλαυκῶπις Ἀθήνη
Οὔλυμπόνδ', ὅθι φασὶ θεῶν ἕδος ἀσφαλὲς αἰεὶ
ἔμμεναι· οὔτ' ἀνέμοισι τινάσσεται οὔτε ποτ' ὄμβρῳ
δεύεται οὔτε χιὼν ἐπιπίλναται ἀλλὰ μάλ' αἴθρη
πέπταται ἀνέφελος, λευκὴ δ' ἐπιδέδρομεν αἴγλη.

Odyssey 6 41-5

apparet diuum numen sedesque quietae,
quas neque concutiunt uenti nec nubila nimbis
aspergunt neque nix acri concreta pruina
cana cadens uiolat semperque innubilus aether
integit et large diffuso lumine ridet.

Lucretius 3 18-22

The divine gods come into view and their peaceful abode which the winds do not shake nor the clouds spatter with rain, nor is it violated by the white falling snow which has been hardened by sharp frost, and it is always covered by pure and cloudless aether and laughs in the broad light which bathes it.

'Superb as Lucretius' version is', writes Farrington 33, 'it will be found in one or two particulars to fall short of the Greek'. In Farrington's very sensitive comparison, he praises the rhythmic qualities of the Lucretius: I note that the run-on lines correspond to the shape of the Greek; the very sound of the Greek has been Latinized, the complex alliterations of the Greek for instance becoming broader and more obvious in the Lucretius. The only technical flaw in the Lucretius, and it is not a serious one, is the repetition *nubila* and *innubilus*. One of the miracles of the Homer is its simplicity, but Farrington is too severe on Lucretius for his failure to attain this. 'In the phrase *large diffuso lumine ridet*, Lucretius employs a metaphor, and thus mars the simplicity of Homer, with whom every word is to be understood literally. Still worse is the phrase *nix acri concreta pruina cana cadens uiolat*, for the words *acri concreta pruina* are padding and *uiolat* substitutes a valuation of the snow-fall for the magic but perfectly literal ἐπιπίλναται'. To the first charge Lucretius might reply, that ἐπιδέδρομεν is a metaphor, too. If light has feet, the *aether* can surely have a face. But even so there is something in the indictment. The Homer is as clean as the sky, despite his running light, whereas Lucretius was an inveterate anthropomorphizer, writing about the phenomena of nature in living human terms. He could plead in extenuation only that it is a strange critique which condemns a poet for using metaphors. If only more poets could produce botches like *large diffuso lumine ridet*. As to the padding, here again Lucretius is being damned for not being what he is not trying to be. He could never be a slavish imitator of Homer or Ennius. When he took his inspiration from them, he shaped what he took in the mould of his own imagination. He was possessed by a passionate interest in meteorological phenomena. He was a fanatical Epicurean. His senses were preternaturally acute. Homer writes 'It is never wet with rain', and this is perfect; but Lucretius is interested in rain and how it is produced and cannot check himself from seeing and hearing how it falls, so he writes 'the clouds do not sprinkle it with rain', *nubila nimbis aspergunt*, even although this extra vizualisa-tion of clouds does land him in difficulties with *innubilus* two lines later. Homer writes 'the snow does not come near it', and this is perfect; but Lucretius is interested in snow and he knows that Epicurus explained it as moisture hardened by the powerful pressure of cold round about it (Diogenes Laertius 10 107), so he writes 'snow which is made hard by sharp frost' *nix acri concreta pruina*. This is not padding, but the fanatical intellectuality which is part of his nature and his power. Similarly, Homer's snow 'comes near', Lucretius' 'violates'. This is partly the anthro-pomorphizer at work, Lucretius thinking of natural phenomena in human terms, in this case in strenuous moral terms. But in this case too we must think of the context. He has just referred to the Epicurean explanation of the origin of snow. Snow is *concreta*. He now visualizes what is *concreta* bombarding the intangibly delicate abode of the gods (see 5 150-4). 'Handle it like a snowflake', we say. But in this context in Lucretius' visualization, snowflakes have become cannon balls. According to Cyril Bailey in his lecture to the British Academy the two primary characteristics of Lucretius were his passion and his *visualization* (and his acute sensory awareness is not confined to vision). Once he has thought of snow being hard, he then shudders at its impact.

Although Wormell in Dudley 45 is inclined to prefer the Lucretius, and puts up a strong case for it, and although it has its own incomparable qualities, I feel that Homer makes a mockery of all imitation, translation, or criticism. Lucretius doesn't come near him. Nobody ever has. This is not a shortcoming in a poet, but an inescapable element in the human condition.

The idea that there is something wrong with the 'meta-phors which Lucretius found ready-made in earlier writers' has led us into something of a digression. As we return to our study of imagery we should remember that Lucretius admired three poets, and two of these were the greatest epic poets that had yet written, *unus Homerus sceptra potitus*, 3 1037-8, and

Ennius . . . noster . . . qui primus amoeno
detulit ex Helicone perenni fronde coronam
per gentis Italas hominum quae clara clueret.
   1 117-9[4]

Our Ennius who was first to take down from lovely Helicon a garland of everlasting green to win bright fame amongst the men of the Italian race.

The third poet whom Lucretius admired (1 729-33) was

4

Empedocles, the greatest of all Greek didactic poets. 'Show me a man's books and I shall tell you his character', they say. These are Lucretius' books and there is nothing that can be objected to in what he read or how he used it.

4. The Theatre and Transfusion of Terms

'What's this, Epicurus? You go to the theatre first thing in the morning to hear them singing to the cithara and the aulos . . . ?' Plutarch.

¶ *Theatrical After-images*
For when in bed we rest our weary limbs,
The mind unburden'd sports in various whims:
The busy head with mimic art runs o'er
The scenes and actions of the day before.
    . . .
The soldier smiling hears the widow's cries,
And stabs the son before the mother's eyes.
With like remorse his brother of the trade,
The butcher, fells the lamb beneath his blade.
    . . .
Orphans around his bed the lawyer sees,
And takes the plaintiff's and defendant's fees.
His fellow pick-purse, watching for a job,
Fancies his fingers in the cully's fob.
    Swift *On Dreams*
This is an imitation of Petronius *fragment* 30, and the Petronius in its turn is based upon Lucretius. All three poems expound the same theory that our dreams are often extrapolations of our waking interests (Lucretius 4 962-5), and each supports the theory by a series of *exempla*. Of the fourteen regularly-patterned couplets of *exempla* in the English poem I have reproduced above only four, to con-trast the slyness and bitterness of Swift as he picks off his targets in even bursts of destructive fire, with the greater freedom and benignity of Lucretius. He too starts with three even, end-stopped lines, the barrister, the

general, the sailor, but then is under way with an interesting
personal statement about his own dreams (brief as such
statements must be if they are to be tolerable) followed by
a lengthy evocation of the dreams and waking after-
images of the theatre-goer:

causidici causas agere et componere leges,
induperatores pugnare ac proelia obire,
nautae contractum cum uentis degere bellum,
nos agere hoc autem et naturam quaerere rerum,
semper et inuentam patriis exponere chartis.   970
    cetera sic studia atque artes plerumque uidentur
in somnis animos hominum frustrata tenere.
et qui cumque dies multos ex ordine ludis
adsiduas dederunt operas, plerumque uidemus,
cum iam destiterunt ea sensibus usurpare,   975
relicuas tamen esse uias in mente patentis,
qua possint eadem rerum simulacra uenire;
per multos itaque illa dies eadem obuersantur
ante oculos, etiam uigilantes ut uideantur
cernere saltantis et mollia membra mouentis   980
et citharae liquidum carmen chordasque loquentis
auribus accipere, et consessum cernere eundem
scenaique simul uarios splendere decores.

    4 966-983

*Barristers dream that they are conducting cases and pitting
law against law; generals fighting and exposing themselves
to battle; sailors waging the war they have undertaken
against the winds; I for my part dream that I am engaged
on this poem, always searching for the truth and when I
find it expounding it in my native language. So all other
vocations and interests very often seem to subject men's minds
to delusions in sleep. If anyone is a constant spectator at the
theatre for days on end, we very often see that when these
spectacles have ceased to occupy his senses, nevertheless there
remain in his mind passages by which images of these same*

*things can approach. And so for many many days the same
sights pass before his eyes so that even when he is awake he
seems to see the dancers moving their lithe bodies and to hear
the speaking strings and liquid song of the harp, and to
see the brilliance of the same audience and the varied beauties
of the stage.*

It is an act of self-denial to stop the Lucretius here as it
moves on to its brilliant descriptions of the dreams of
hunting dogs and race horses and birds and kings, then the
guilt dreams, the dreams of falling and of thirst and lastly,
bedwetting and wet dreams. For Lucretius will make
poetry out of anything and bend anything to its will. It is
quite in his manner so to drag down his own poetic afflatus.
The most striking of these acts of violence occurs earlier in
this book where he is discussing the workings of the olfac-
tory sense. 'Bees', he says as any poet might, 'are attracted
enormous distances by the odour of honey', and adds as few
poets would, 'and vultures by corpses':

mellis apes quamius longe ducuntur odore,
uolturiique cadaueribus.

4 679-80

Self-denial operating, we return to the lawyers and
generals (966-7). Here we may suspect from the three end-
stopped lines that Lucretius has been forced into some padding, but not for long. *Degere bellum* in 968 teases the mind
by transferring the general's wars to the sailor's storms,
but *contractum degere* 'to carry on (in their dreams) the
war they have undertaken', carries yet another suggestion.
Here I think Lucretius is hinting at a nautical detail.
Contractum is a striking word. A sailor rides out a storm
contractis uelis taking in sail. So I think there may be just a
hint of a double reference. The sailors are waging the war
they have *contracted* – a *contracted* war with the winds.

But even if these *exempla* are routine, Lucretius soon
leaves them for something personal. He has already disclosed

in his great proem in the first book that he is a night worker
(1 142-4). Here he reveals that even when he does go
to bed the *De Rerum Natura* is still churning in his brain.
Anybody who studies languages will respond to *patriis
exponere chartis.* He is hunting out the truth in Greek
philosophical writings and expounding it in Latin. Even
scholars dream superb linguistic discoveries, although they
do not often survive the dawn critique. Lucretius offers no
pompous apology for citing his own experience, but is
modest and matter-of-fact about it. *Cetera sic studia*
suggests that he's just like everybody else.

The passage that follows is remarkable for its picture of
an Italian theatre show, and of the man who is mad on the
theatre, so mad that not just his dreams, but even his
waking after-images visual and aural, are full of its glitter
and excitement.

¶ *Colour in the Theatre.* This apparent interest in the
theatre occurs in similar terms at the beginning of the
fourth book where he is expounding his optical theory. To
prove that all objects give off a fine film of particles from
their outermost surface, he cites the analogy of the colour
given off by the canvas awnings used as overhead protection
in open-air theatres:

> et uolgo faciunt id lutea russaque uela
> et ferrugina, cum magnis intenta theatris
> per malos uolgata trabesque trementia flutant;
> namque ibi consessum caueai supter et omnem
> scaenai speciem patrum matrumque decorem
> inficiunt coguntque suo fluitare colore.
> et quanto circum mage sunt inclusa theatri
> moenia, tam magis haec intus perfusa lepore
> omnia conrident correpta luce diei.
>   4 75-83

*This often happens with yellow, red and purple canvasses
spread tight over masts and beams in great theatres. For as*

they tremble and ripple, they dye the auditorium beneath them, and the whole spectacle of the stage, the magnificent array of senators and of matrons, making everything ripple with their colours; and the more they enclose the walls of the theatre, the more the daylight is reduced and everything inside the walls is bathed in their smiling beauty.

Lucretius' visual sense is active in his reference to the masts and beams on which the awnings are supported, and in the image whereby the canvas is said to undulate, *fluitare*, a word used properly of water. This imagery is put to vigorous logical work carrying a whole theory of optics, when the undulating awnings are said to make the audience undulate with colour. That is to say that as the canvasses undulate they cast off waves of colour particles which fall on the people below them, and rebound to the eye of the beholder to be received as waves of colour. This water image is caught up in *perfusa lepore*, soaked in beauty. The end of the quotation shows Lucretius following up his interest in the technical details of architecture. Robertson de-scribing the Roman-type theatre at Aspendus notes that 'the *scaena* is as high as the *cauea* to which it is united'. If then the walls of the bowl of a Roman theatre are about the same height as the stage buildings, the more the walls of the theatre are enclosed all round, that is, the fewer chinks there are between the awnings and the top of the theatre walls, the more intensely will everything inside the theatre be saturated with colour as the direct daylight is diminished.

Textual critics have been needlessly dismayed by the fathers and mothers in this scene. Surely they are mentioned because the whiteness of the senators' togas and the splen-dour of the matrons' finery would provide the most striking colour effects under the coloured awnings. Besides, the senators all sat together at the front and must have formed an impressive spectacle. They caught the eye of Virgil, for instance, in his description of the prototype of such a theatre:

hic totum caueae consessum ingentis et ora
prima patrum magnis Salius clamoribus implet.
Aeneid 5 340-1
Then Salius filled with his loud protests the whole vast
bowl of seats and the faces of the fathers at the front.

To his shouts I should like to add my own on seeing how the
Penguin translation glozes over the zeugma with *implet.*
'He filled the whole auditorium and the faces of the fathers
sitting at the front' is in essence what Virgil says, and this
paraphrase shows how the same verb is used in two slightly
different senses with two different objects, the poetic result
being that we are suddenly made to see with Salius' eyes
the staring faces in the front row. This is utterly Virgilian,
and like so much in Virgil utterly saturated in Lucretius.
The very choice of the word *implet* may have been prompted
by the watery connotation of *fluitare* and *perfusa* in our
passage. But none of this is imaginable in the uneventful
texture of Jackson Knight's translation:

'At this Salius shouted his protests to the elders in
the front rows and all who were sitting in the vast
amphitheatre.'

Matrons are equally conspicuous in the theatre for different reasons. Terence in his prologue to the *Hecyra* reveals
that the shrieking of women helped to ruin the play's
first performance. Ovid advises on the other hand the lover
to look for a mistress in the auditorium of the theatre:

ut redit itque frequens longum formica per agmen,
    granifero solitum cum uehit ore cibum,
aut ut apes saltusque suos et olentia nactae   95
    pascua per flores et thyma summa uolant,
sic ruit ad celebres cultissima femina ludos;
    copia iudicium saepe morata meum est.
spectatum ueniunt, ueniunt spectentur ut ipsae.

Ars Amatoria 1 93-99

As throngs of ants come and go in long columns carrying
the grain that is their normal food in their mouths; or as
bees take possession of their favourite groves and scented
feeding grounds, flying amongst the heads of the flowers and
the thyme; so do women rush in all their finery to congregate
at the games in such numbers that I have often found it
difficult to choose quickly between them. They come to see.
They also come in order to be seen.

¶ *Crowds.* Crowd management is a problem at.sports arenas
and theatres. Lucretius makes a clear reference to this
difficulty in proving that all sounds, including the human
voice, are composed of material particles:

praeterea radit uox fauces saepe facitque
asperiora foras gradiens arteria clamor,
quippe per angustum turba maiore coorta   530
ire foras ubi coeperunt primordia uocum,
scilicet expleti quoque ianua raditur oris.
haud igitur dubiumst quin uoces uerbaque constent
corporeis e principiis, ut laedere possint.

4 528-34

In addition the voice often scrapes the throat and shouting
makes the windpipe rougher on its way out. For when the
particles of voice form a larger crowd than usual and start
to emerge through the narrow exit obviously the crowded
doorway of the mouth is scraped also. Thus, since voice and
words can do damage, there is no doubt that they are com-
posed of material particles.

The argument takes a surprising twist here. We should
expect Lucretius to say that the shouting voice scrapes the
throat like a crowd of people scraping gateposts on their
way out. Therefore the voice is corporeal, since it can inflict
physical damage. But this simple analogical argument is not
what Lucretius provides. 'The shouting voice scrapes the
throat,' he says, 'for when the particles of voice form a
crowd and start to come out through the narrow passage,

clearly the doorway of the crowded mouth is scraped also'
(that is to say like the doorway of a crowded passage). In
this sentence argument and metaphor coalesce. What he
writes is a conflation of (*a*) the narrow opening of the
crowded mouth is scraped and (*b*) the opening of the mouth
is scraped just as a narrow exit of a crowded passage is
scraped. I have laboured the exact logic of this word 'also',
because it seems to me to be blurred or misunderstood in
most of the translations, and also because it is of some
importance for our understanding of Lucretius' intelligence.
The general impact of this argument is unmistakable, and it
is driven home by correspondences in the language: *raditur*
answers to *radit*, *per angustum* to *arteria*, *ire foras* to *foras
gradiens* and *turba maior* to *clamor*, shouting being a concentration of many physical particles (cf. 539-41). To enforce the argument Lucretius almost resorts to puns: *fauces* is
often applied in an architectural sense to a passage (the
modern architect might call it a vomitory); *arteria* carries
with it the connotation of *artus*, 'narrow'; and *oris* is as ambivalent as the English word mouth. But the extreme inter-
change is with *ianua*, applied by Lucretius and only here in
Latin to part of the human throat. The doorway of the
crowded mouth is a metaphor created and explained by the
content of the argument. All of these linguistic details illustrate the vivacity of Lucretius' senses and imagination, but
there is another important point of Lucretian practice to be
detected in this extract. Judged as an exposition of a philosophical argument it is unsatisfactory, because of the vacill-
ation between literal and metaphorical expression. This inter-
fusion of the proposition which he is trying to prove and
the image by which he illustrates it has caused considerable
difficulty to commentators and translators. Pedagogically
this is not as it should be. The pedagogue has been over-
borne by the poet. This reckless fusing of the metaphorical
and the literal, which would be inexcusable in a textbook

is another example of the unrestrainable visualizing which is the source of so much energy and excitement in this poetry. It is not a question of lack of intelligence. The formal argument is simple, so simple and easy to grasp that the poet's imagination runs away with it, abandoning the obvious systematic exposition for the metaphor, straining after all the detailed resemblances which flash before it. The confusion is one which troubles the analyst only; the disciple will be swept along by the tide of the argument, and such is its power that nobody cares about, or even notices, a central weakness in it, that a crowd does not roughen doorways but wears them smooth.

¶ *Cockcrow.* After these thorny examples it would be pleasant to leave the theatre with a more direct and simple image. *Explaudere* is a technical term for driving actors ignominiously off the stage by clapping the hands. It is often used metaphorically but never with such panache as by Lucretius, with the juxtaposition *auroram clara* exploiting the double reference of *clara*, to the eyes as well as the ears, and also, as Yvan Nadeau points out to me, the appeal for loud applause which ends five of Plautus' comedies, like *clare plaudite* at the end of the *Amphitruo*:

... gallum noctem explaudentibus alis
auroram clara consuetum uoce uocare.

4 710-1

the cock who drives night off the stage by flapping his wings and summons the morning with his bright voice.

¶ *Transfusion of Terms.* This chapter has provided additional illustrations of the characteristics which we have already found in Lucretius' images, the acuity of their detail, their dialectical validity and their abundance. In addition the repeated rippling and the dyeing and the soaking in the optical discussion from the beginning of the fourth book show that the poet can use a related image several times in slightly different logical relationships in the same passage. We shall postpone treatment of this until a later chapter but here we discuss the characteristic we noticed in the passage about the voice 4 528-34. There the terms of the analogy were not kept systematically distinct from the terms of his literal argument. This 'transfusion' of terms can be exemplified from other passages.

If you held a torch over the cold spring at Dodona, it would burst into flame. And if you dropped it into the spring it would continue to burn in the water. In the sixth book Lucretius explains this phenomenon in atomic terms. In the spring there are many *seeds* of heat which gather and rise from the water so that fire is *conceived, semina* 884 picking up *concepto* 880. As an analogy for those who find this implausible Lucretius cites the fresh water springs which rise in the salt sea. And now comes the transfusion:

sic igitur per eum possunt erumpere fontem
et scatere illa foras in stuppam semina.

    6 895-6

This is how seeds of fire can burst out of the fountain of Dodona and overflow on to the torch.

Scatere is a verb normally applied to liquids welling up (5 952), but here transposed from the analogy of fresh water to Lucretius' proposition about the seeds of heat in the water.

With characteristic generosity Lucretius now produces another analogy. If you put out a torch, and then move it close to a burning torch, it will ignite before it touches the flame:

multaque praeterea prius ipso tacta uapore
eminus ardescunt quam comminus imbuat ignis.
hoc igitur fieri quoque in illo fonte putandumst.

    6 903-5

And many other things burst into flame at a distance when they are touched just by the heat, before coming close and being dipped in the fire. So we must suppose that this is what is happening with the fountain at Dodona.

Imbuat implies that the fire moistens. The liquid term from the first analogy has spilled over, this time not on to the argument proper but on to the next analogy.

Similarly, in the list of great men who have succumbed to death:

ipse Epicurus obit decurso lumine uitae,

qui genus humanum ingenio superauit et omnes

restinxit stellas exortus ut aetherius sol.

3 1042 - 4

Even Epicurus died when the light of his life had set, and he surpassed with his genius the whole human race and dimmed all men as the heavenly sun dims the stars at its rising. Here although the comparison is not explicit till the mention of the sun in the last word of the sentence, the death and the excellence of Epicurus are both expressed in terms applicable to the sun. At *obire* my translation gives up in despair. Apart from being used of human beings dying, it often refers to the setting of heavenly bodies, but I have put that all into *decurso*[5] which is used in similar contexts even as early as *exorto iubare, noctis decurso itinere* in Pacuvius, *tragicorum fragmenta* 347R, 'when the brilliant sun arose and the journey of the night has run down the sky'. But the difficulty is with *restinxit*. To say *in uacuo* that Epicurus extinguished all other men, doesn't make sense. *Restinguere* is not used in the sense of 'surpass' or 'outclass' except in this sentence where the term drifts in from the simile.

A last example of this transfusion of terms between the image and the literal context occurs where Lucretius is arguing that there are no tortures awaiting us in the underworld. Then he mentions punishments on the earth and our fears of their continuance in the afterlife:

uerbera carnifices robur pix lammina taedae;

quae tamen etsi absunt, at mens sibi conscia factis

praemetuens adhibet stimulos torretque flagellis.

3 1017- 9

lashes, executioners, prison, pitch, metal plates, burning
torches; even if these are absent, none the less the mind
deeply conscious of its own guilt, in fear for the future
applies the goad and tortures itself with lashes.
The best editors of Lucretius emend *torretque* in 1019
because it is not a word applied to lashings. The lash is
normally said *urere*, never *torrere*. On the other hand, as
Bailey sees, *torrere* is frequently used of mental anguish. So
here in the middle of his metaphor of goads and lashes he
uses a verb which strictly applies only to his literal subject,
the mind. But as *imbuat* in our first example (6 879-905, see
pp. 44-5) referred not to the literal context but to the first
analogy, so too here *torrere* may also glance back at the
pix lammina taedae, the real scorching instruments which
have just been mentioned.

In view of recent discussions by Turner and Spencer of the
debt of Shelley to Lucretius it may be interesting to point
out the resemblance between line 1017 just quoted and

with thumbscrews, wheels, with tooth and spike and jag.
                                                    Shelley
And the differences. The rhetoric of the English lies partly
in the repetition of 'with' and 'and'. In the Latin there are
no such words. Asyndetic lists of this sort are extremely
common in early Latin poetry, half-a-dozen such lines
occurring for instance, in the first four hundred lines of the
fragments of Lucilius.

Such transfusions are so commonplace in literature that
they may be felt to be hardly worth noting. But I believe
that the observation will help us to see more of what the
poetry is doing in more difficult passages in Lucretius.

At the end of the first book for instance, Lucretius is
attacking the idea that the universe is finite. 'If it is', he
says, 'let a man go to its boundaries and throw a javelin.
Will it go on outside the universe or will something block
its flight?'

alterutrum fatearis enim sumasque necessest.
quorum utrumque tibi effugium praecludit et omne   975
cogit ut exempta concedas fine patere.
nam siue est aliquid quod probeat efficiatque
quo minus quo missum est ueniat finique locet se,
siue foras fertur, non est a fine profectum.
hoc pacto sequar atque, oras ubi cumque locaris   980
extremas, quaeram quid telo denique fiat:
fiet uti nusquam possit consistere finis
effugiumque fugae prolatet copia semper.
1 974-983
*You must concede and assume one or the other. But each
of them blocks your escape and compels you to admit that
the universe extends without limit. For whether there is
something which effectively prevents it from reaching the
point it was aimed at and arriving at its limit, or whether it
flies out of the universe, in neither case has it started from the
limit. In this way I shall follow you and wherever you put
the ultimate boundary, I shall ask you what then happens
to the javelin. What will happen is that no limit can be
established anywhere and that room for flight extends the
possibility of flying.*

This translation is rather spiky but so is the Latin, and
mainly because of the tangling of the terms *finis* limit, and
effugium escape. *Finis* in 976 and 979 means 'boundary'.
In 978 it refers to the javelin's target and the translators
lose this by using a different word or omitting the whole
phrase. In 975 the believer in the finite universe has his
escape, *effugium*, blocked in front of him by a dilemma. In
983 the abundance of space to fly in prolongs the possibility
of escape, *effugium*, for the javelin. This is such a strange
transfusion of terms that Latham takes refuge in Giussani's
interpretation, 'final escape from this conclusion is pre-
cluded by the limitless possibility of running away from it'.
All this, and the two different senses of *fiat* and *fiet* in

981 and 982, were seen by Munro, and subsequent translations and commentaries exhibit a decline in the understanding of these features which are essential to the
understanding of the poetry. What is Lucretian here is
the immediacy with which Lucretius conveys his persistent
pursuit of the man with the javelin. It is clearly a javelin
or spear because as it is hurled a rifling is imparted to it by
a leather thong, *ualidis contortum uiribus* (971), and because
this is a clear reference to the formal declaration of war
whereby the Roman fetial hurled his spear over the enemy
frontier – and yet there are still English translators trifling
with darts. This immediacy which is the hallmark of
Lucretius is heightened by the transfusions of terms. As
Lucretius describes how the man with the javelin takes up
one stance after another out into infinity, so *finis, effugium*,
and *fieri* change their meanings. That this weird correspondence is deliberate and effective, we shall try to argue
in the last chapter of this book.

5. Games and Double images

'The wise man will take greater pleasure than other people in public shows.' Epicurus.

This chapter will study a few more images, some of them concerned with games, and move on from these studies to a consideration of double images.

¶ *The Torch Race.* One of the most thrilling sporting events in classical Athens must have been the relay torch race, as run, for example, at the Panathenaic Festival. On a summer night, after days of celebration, of feasting and processions, teams representing five of the ten tribes of Athens raced the 1,000 metres from Dipylon gate to the altar of Pro-metheus. Each team consisted of forty runners, each run-ning 25 metres. Thirty-nine torch changes at full sprint in each of the five teams provided one hundred and ninety-five ocasions to raise or dash the hopes of spectators, as their representatives hurled themselves along the dark streets. Add to all this the local pride and patriotism, the religious emotion and drinking involved, and we have a mixture which must have made a rousing night of it.

All this had been defunct for many years before Lucretius wrote, but he does refer to the same kind of race in a short simile at the end of his discussion of the impermanence of all things. His argument is that the birth and death of everything, its blooming and its ageing, all are to be explained in terms of the eternal restlessness of the com-ponent atoms:

...sic rerum summa nouatur

semper, et inter se mortales mutua uiuunt.

augescunt aliae gentes, aliae minuuntur,

inque breui spatio mutantur saecla animantum
et quasi cursores uitai lampada tradunt.

2 75-9

*So is the sum of things eternally renewed and all living
creatures live off each other. Some communities increase
while others decline and after a brief course the generations
of the living are changed, and like runners hand over the
torch of life.*

The runners are the generations. Their torch is life. They
hand it on, so they are runners in a relay torch race. Each
has a short lap to run (*spatio*, a race course, touches the
image but it is not easy for the translator to catch it
deftly enough). So much for explicit resemblances between
this deeply-moving simile and the deeply-moving argument which it crowns. But it may be that part of the effect
of all this upon us lies in the unmentioned resemblances
which we are left to explore, the darkness in which the
runner waits, the strenuousness and brevity of his effort,
his exhaustion at the end of his distance, the darkness into
which he returns when the race passes him by. And perhaps
even the differences. This race is a longer and vaster enter-
prise than any torch race, and there is no camaraderie
after it, no disappointment in defeat, no glory for anybody,
no amphora of oil for the first man home. The runners are
broken up to make their successors.

This type of race is lightly alluded to when Lucretius is
telling the story of Phaethon. Lucretius makes it quite
clear that he doesn't believe in such myths. In the context
in the fifth book he is arguing that our world is an imper-
manent equipoise of warring forces. In time of flood we see
water gaining the upper hand; during heat-waves, fire is
threatening to overwhelm everything. He steps aside from
this argument for a moment to discount mythology, to
explain that this is the explanation of the story of
Phaethon:

ignis enim superauit et ambiens multa perussit,
auia cum Phaethonta rapax uis solis equorum
aethere raptauit toto terrasque per omnis.
at pater omnipotens ira tum percitus acri
magnanimum Phaethonta repenti fulminis ictu   400
deturbauit equis in terram, Solque cadenti
obuius aeternam succepit lampada mundi
disiectosque redegit equos iunxitque trementis,
inde suum per iter recreauit cuncta gubernans,
scilicet ut ueteres Graium cecinere poetae.   405
   quod procul a uera nimis est ratione repulsum.
ignis enim superare potest ubi materiai
ex infinito sunt corpora plura coorta;
inde cadunt uires aliqua ratione reuictae,
aut pereunt res exustae torrentibus auris.

5 396 - 410

*For fire was victorious and went round scorching many
parts of the earth, when the whirling force of the horses of the
sun bolted, and hurled Phaethon all over the sky and over
all the countries of the earth. This roused omnipotent
Jupiter to fierce wrath and with a sudden thunderbolt he
struck great-hearted Phaethon down from his horses to the
ground, and the god of the sun came to meet him as he fell
and took over the eternal torch of the world, bringing to rein
again the scattered horses yoking them as they trembled.
Then he drove them over their proper course and renewed all
life, – that at any rate is the tale of the old Greek poets, but it
is far, far removed from the true account. For fire can be
victorious when an unusually great number of the bodies of
fire gather together out of the infinite; then either its strength
falls overcome by some means or else things perish burned
up by its scorching blasts.*

This is an allegory. The ungovernable horses carried
Phaethon *all* over the sky and the earth; that is, heat went
round scorching *many* parts of the earth (*terrasque per*

omnis, cf. *ambiens multa perussit*). So again when the god of the sun gets the horses in hand he drives them over their proper course restoring *everything* (*suum per iter recreauit cuncta*). This shows that *ambiens multa* is doubly dovetailed into the context and tells heavily against the other reading *lambens multa*. Flames do lick in Latin, though not in Lucretius – (*degustant tigna trabesque* 2 192 is the nearest), but it is unlikely that they are licking here, making an extraneous image, while *ambiens* has this double logical bedding in the context. Bailey is therefore wrong is saying that the meaning of *ambiens* is a little feeble. It is accurate and active in the argument, whereas *lambens* is suspiciously decorative. Emendators of Lucretius often titivate the true text, as for example when they throw out *remouet* 2 199 and substitute the journalistic *reuomit* (see West 97).

There can be no mistaking the logical structure of this passage. We have a statement of the literal fact in the first line (396), followed by the mythological allegory of it (397-404). Then we are explicitly told that this is an allegorical fiction (405-6) and lines 407-10 are a restate-ment of the literal fact. Just as *ambiens multa perussit* in the first line interlocks with the allegorical *terras per omnis* and *recreauit cuncta*, so in the restatement *ignis enim superare* and *inde cadunt uires . . . reuictae* clearly interlock with *ignis enim superauit* and with lines 400-1 of the myth.

In this passage Lucretius employs several apparently ornamental epithets in the epic manner. In the light of our discussion of such epithets at the end of chapter three, we should look closely at their function in this context. The whole passage is highly wrought. It is the *whirling* might of the horses of the sun that *whirls* Phaethon away (*rapax . . . raptauit*)[6], and here in the first line of the myth we have not only this instance of *figura etymologica*, but also the epic periphrasis with *uis*, like for example *odora canum uis* meaning 'hunting dogs' in Virgil *Aeneid* 4 132. It is a *sharp* anger that rouses Zeus. He is *almighty* and the lamp of the world is *everlasting*, both in defiance of Epicurean dogma. Phaethon is *great-hearted*, not that Lucretius is raising serious sympathy for this shadowy figure in a false myth but his escapade is sufficiently like the more successful exploits of Epicurus (1 72-4), to earn this passing accolade. The *trembling* of horses as they are being strapped in between the shafts *after* recovering from a stampede, is just the significant detail that Lucretius would seize upon, and it is tantalizing to see the waste of it in Latham's translation which spoils the picture by running two operations into one, 'brought the trembling steeds back to the yoke from their stampede'.

The elevation of tone arouses some suspicion that Lucretius may be parodying the style of Epic narrative. The suspicion is confirmed, and the purpose of the parody is explained in lines 405-6 '. . . at any rate according to the utterances of the ancient Greek poets, which are very far removed from the truth'. The sarcastic *scilicet* makes it quite obvious that Lucretius is up to his old trick of lightly mimicking the tone of voice of those with whom he disagrees.

The allusion to the torch race, if there is one, occurs in line 402. When Jupiter knocks Phaethon down with a thunderbolt, his father takes over the chariot of the sun. The first runner is falling (*cadenti*), his successor meets him (*obvius*), and takes over the torch (*succepit lampada*). But this is no normal torch. It is the inextinguishable torch of the world. Here again we find poetic effects in differences between the image and the illustrandum. The relay torch eventually will be spent, not so the sun: the runner stumbles but Phaethon is knocked out of the sky by a thunderbolt; his successor who picks the torch out of his hands is his own father; in a relay race the runner who has finished his run, gets his breath back and walks away, but after this torch change Phaethon falls to his death.

¶ *Caged Animals.* McKay has recently thrown great light upon the astonishing passage discussed on page 20 by show-ing that Lucretius may well have witnessed animal fights in the amphitheatre. There may be another trace of these which has not been fully elucidated. In 6 173-203 Lucretius is arguing that lightning is generated when winds are trapped within great heaped-up cloud structures above our head.

> tum poteris magnas moles cognoscere eorum
> speluncasque uel ut saxis pendentibus structas   195
> cernere, quas uenti cum tempestate coorta
> conplerunt, magno indignantur murmure clausi
> nubibus in caueisque ferarum more minantur,
> nunc hinc nunc illinc fremitus per nubila mittunt,
> quaerentesque uiam circum uersantur . . .
>   6 194-200

Then you will be able to see their great structures, and pick out the caves apparently built of hanging rocks. These the winds fill when the storm rises, and then imprisoned in the clouds they rage with a loud grumbling and bluster like wild beasts shut up in cages, sending their roars now this way now that through the clouds, and circling around looking for a way out . . .

Munro notices that *fremitus* in 199 keeps up the illustra-tion of wild beasts, and Bailey rewords his note. This is surely not enough. The winds in the clouds are like beasts in their cages. So nobody should be able to read *nunc hinc nunc illinc* without thinking of the despairing creatures pacing to and fro in their cages in Rome like the cheetah in the Edinburgh Zoo. Lucretius tells us explicitly that winds shut up in clouds roar like wild beasts in cages. In the very next line *nunc hinc nunc illinc fremitus per nubila mittunt,* Munro sees that the roaring of the winds is like the roaring of animals, but we are surely comatose if we do not see that the movement of the winds is the pacing of the animals, and also that the roaring of the winds through the clouds is the roaring of the animals through the bars.

¶ *Horses.* These and other passages (for example, 4 989-90, 6 92-5), suggest that Lucretius took an interest in such sports, and there is certainly no doubt of his interest in animals. Horses are detected by Masson 161 in the fifth book where 'the trees of various kinds run a race with each other, like horses speeding at full gallop':

arboribusque datumst uariis exinde per auras
crescendi magnum inmissis certamen habenis.

5 786-7

There is another horse, which has been much less clearly visualized by some scholars:

denique ubi in medio nobis ecus acer obhaesit
flumine et in rapidas amnis despeximus undas,
stantis equi corpus transuersum ferre uidetur
uis et in aduersum flumen contrudere raptim,
et quo cumque oculos traiecimus omnia ferri
et fluere adsimili nobis ratione uidentur.

4 420-5

Then when our spirited horse sticks in midstream and we look down into the swirling waters of the river, although the horse is standing still it looks as though the current is carrying it sideways and thrusting it hard upstream, and wherever we turn our eyes everything seems to be carried along flowing in the same direction as ourselves.

The horse seems to be carried sideways, *transuersum,* a vivid detail because it brings irresistibly before the eyes the horse stuck side on to the current with the weight of the water striking its flank, but Ernout's translation misses it out, Leonard offers 'reversely from his course', and Latham 'seems to be breasting the flood'. Again in the last line of the passage, *adsimili nobis ratione* (cf. *eadem aliis quiete* 3 1038) suggests that all the visible objects on the bank appear to be moving in the same direction as the rider, surely upstream, but Bailey 1227 sees everything else 'flowing down with us'.

If scholars were unable to visualize this situation a moment's experiment would have shown them what was meant.
Better to drown in the nearest river than make such a mess
of the poetry. It is time Lucretius were rescued from the
sensory torpor of the study and brought out into the fresh air.
At the beginning of the second book free will is connected
with the swerve of the atoms. In 263-5 the race course
provides an analogy and we see the horses bursting from
their traps *patefactis tempore puncto carceribus*. In 272-5
our body is carried along against our will by the movement
of some external force, presumably a crowd, until in 276 it
is checked by the bit (*refrenauit*) of our will. In 277-80
again we see a crowd moving forward against its will,
often rushing out of control, although there is something
within our breasts fighting against it. Now back again we
go to the horse metaphor, for at the discretion of this thing
inside us, our bodies can be steered and when they have
been hurled forward can be reined in and made to settle
back down again (*flecti, refrenatur, retro residit*).

This is a difficult passage, and it is not within the scope
of this book to attempt a full acount of it. But this brief
glimpse at its imagery shows how Lucretius can use a
double image, going backwards and forwards from race
horses to a crowd. The double image is the general characteristic[7] with which we shall end this chapter.

¶ *Double Images.* In his atomic explanation of acoustics,
Lucretius is arguing that when we hear a sound, material
particles are actually entering our ears, rough particles if the
sounds are harsh, smooth particles if the sounds are smooth:

nec simili penetrant auris primordia forma,
cum tuba depresso grauiter sub murmure mugit
et reboat raucum regio cita barbara bombum,
et uolucres gelidis nocte hortis ex Heliconis
cum liquidam tollunt lugubri uoce querellam.
4 542-6

*And the particles which enter the ears when the trumpet
roars heavily with its burdened murmur and the places of
the East vibrate in response flinging back its hoarse boom,
are not the same shape as the particles we receive when the
night birds from the chill gardens of Helicon sadly lift up
their liquid lamentations.*

The text of this passage has not yet been securely established
and I have merely transcribed what Diels offers but whatever the truth may be about lines 544-5, there is a clear
double image. To his contrast between roughness and
smoothness, physical and aural, Lucretius has gratuitously
added another by his references to heaviness and lightness,
depresso grauiter and *tollunt*. It is the gratuity of a poet.

A more complex intertwining of metaphors can be studied
in the great attack on superstition in the proem to the first
book:

humana ante oculos foede cum uita iaceret
in terris oppressa graui sub religione,
quae caput a caeli regionibus ostendebat
horribili super aspectu mortalibus instans,   65
primum Graius homo mortalis tendere contra
est oculos ausus primusque obsistere contra;
quem neque fama deum nec fulmina nec minitanti
murmure compressit caelum, sed eo magis acrem
inritat animi uirtutem, effringere ut arta   70
naturae primus portarum claustra cupiret.
ergo uiuida uis animi peruicit et extra
processit longe flammantia moenia mundi
atque omne immensum peragrauit mente animoque,
unde refert nobis uictor quid possit oriri,   75
quid nequeat, finita potestas denique cuique
qua nam sit ratione atque alte terminus haerens.
quare religio pedibus subiecta uicissim
opteritur, nos exaequat uictoria caelo.

1 62-79

When human life lay abjectly grovelling upon the earth under the oppressive weight of religion which showed its head from the direction of the sky, bearing down upon mortals with terrifying face, it was a Greek who was the first man who dared stretch mortal eyes against it, who first dared to stand against religion. He was not repressed by the talk about the gods, by lightning or the threatening murmurs of the sky, but rather these stimulated the sharp courage of his mind to long to be the first to burst the restrictive bolts of the gates of Nature. So the living vigour of his mind won through and he moved out far beyond the flaming walls of the world and traversed the whole immeasurable Universe with his intellect, bringing triumphantly back to us information about what can arise and what cannot, how in short every-thing has its own function defined for it and its deep-set boundary stone. The result is that it is the turn of religion to be trampled underfoot, while his victory raises us up to the sky.

Two images dominate this passage. At the beginning human life is grovelling on the ground under the oppressive weight of religion. Religion is showing its fearsome face from the direction of the sky. This makes a powerful impact because according to Epicurus and Lucretius, the beliefs they were combating were largely inspired by the vast and incompre-hensible phenomena of the sky. This is the philosophical reference of the terror in the sky so often mentioned by Lucretius, for example when 'the hideous cloud of night gathers' at 4 172-3, 'and faces of dark fear hang down over us'. So when Bailey's nerve fails him and he translates *atrae formidinis ora* as 'the shapes of dark fear', he has lost the theology as well as the poetry. Shakespeare does not lose his nerve. In *Antony and Cleopatra* clouds are like dragons, bears, lions, citadels, rocks, promontories and horses.

The theological point is lost also by those who suggest with Wormell (in *Greece and Rome*) that Lucretius was here inspired by Etruscan representations of the demons of Hell. The faces on the urns at Volterra or those reproduced by Pallottino are sufficiently hideous, but it is wrong to invoke them. The face which Lucretius talks about is in the sky and none of the Etruscan ones is. The fear of the sky and particularly the night sky, and sky lowering with clouds, the home of malevolent powers which *stand* over us, *superstitio*, this is the line of thought in Lucretius and is far closer to his main concerns, like the Epicurean objections to the Astral Religion of Plato and Aristotle[8], than are the demons of Etruscan art.

So much for the first four lines of this passage. This image is picked up in the last two lines. 'It is now the turn of religion to be trampled underfoot.' *Uicissim* meaning 'in turn' puts this beyond doubt. In the beginning human life is lying abject under the oppression of religion from the sky. After Epicurus' heroics, the tables are turned (*uicissim*), we are raised to the sky in victory and religion is trampled underfoot.

The seminal article by Davies which raised interest in this passage did not see this, did not even quote or consider the first few lines, without which the last two are incomprehensible. 'The most important aspect of this metaphor', according to Davies and scholars since Davies, 'is the use made of the Roman triumph.' A Roman triumph was the solemn procession of a victorious general into the city of Rome, riding on a chariot, leading booty and chained prisoners, welcomed by a shouting crowd. In our passage there are no chains, no chariot and no shouts. Davies builds up the idea of the triumph on line 75 where Epicurus is said to bring back knowledge to us. 'Epicurus', he writes, 'is a conquering general: he is to conquer the *natura rerum* which is defended by his enemy *religio*. There is a kind of inverted siege, with the attack proceeding outwards instead of inwards – a very typical metaphysical device. The *immensum*, the infinite, is the place where the *natura rerum* is to be found, fortified by the *flammantia moenia*; the attack succeeds, the walls are carried and set on fire (*flammantia*), and a Roman triumph is conferred upon Epicurus. He returns to the city with his spoils, the *natura rerum*, leading his conquered enemy, *religio*, in shameful chains, *obteritur*. Then the whole thing is wound up with *nos exaequat uictoria caelo.*' Davies is reacting with keen feeling to some hints in the Latin, but ends by leaving the Latin far behind. His complete neglect of lines 62-5 has made it impossible for him to understand 78-9, in particular the crucial word *uicissim*. The 'leading' of religion, and her 'shameful chains' are complete inventions, which destroy the oppression image which spans this passage.

Nor is the central portion with its military image anything like so metaphysical as Davies makes out. In lines 70-5 *peruicit* suggests a military picture, *extra moenia processit* clinches it. It is continued on *peragrauit*, which hints at a foraging expedition (Latham has 'voyaging'), and *refert nobis uictor* completes the communiqué. This is the report of an action, not of ceremonial. A patrol going out on a foraging expedition to scour the surrounding countryside might be expected to slip out through a postern in the walls under cover of darkness. But not Epicurus. He burst the bolts of the gates outwards.

In this passage, then, we have a double image, the central military metaphor spanned by the two oppression metaphors merging quite smoothly in lines 67-9 where the oppressor becomes the enemy (*compressit* picking up *oppressa*)[9], and line 78 where the enemy becomes the oppressed.

The main point of this book has been to recommend that terms which are operative in an image should be pointed out so that the reader may be helped to see the interplay between the metaphorical and the literal. For instance the bolts of the gates of nature are said to be narrow in line 70. By a common Latin poetic idiom this may be taken to mean that the gates were narrow. The application to the beleaguered strong point is there for the mind to explore; with reference to Lucretius' literal topic, it is wonderfully suggestive of the narrow confines of man's understanding before Epicurus enlarged it. Until these correspondences are noticed, the poetry cannot be giving the reader any-thing like what the poet was experiencing. When he puts human limitations into correspondence with bolts, if we are to keep up with him we must be stimulated intellectually to explore the resemblance, and stimulated emotionally to feel about the philosophy of Epicurus the excitement and admiration with which Lucretius regarded a brilliant and courageous military success.

There are dangers in this approach. These equations are too schematic. We are always oversimplifying. This is just the basic algebra of what Lucretius wrote and it breaks down because he is not doing algebra. The simple basic pattern is complicated by other vaguer shapes. The deep-set boundary stone in line 77 is less clearly glimpsed than the deep-driven one in 2 1087 *uitae depactus terminus alte*. But despite this and despite the possible thought of in-consistency involved in positing a boundary stone in an immeasurable universe, we should take this in our stride, and see that Lucretius is trying to suggest the certainty and immutable sacrosanctity of Epicurean dogma in terms which would strike deep at Roman religious consciousness, and legal and agricultural traditions.

An even more fleeting image grazes the senses where we read that Epicurus was the first man to stretch mortal eyes against superstition. *Tendere oculos* is a surprising phrase preserved by the fourth-century grammarian Nonius, so surprising that many editors follow the manuscripts and read *tollere oculos*. I think it should surprise us, at the beginning of this military context, into thinking of the stretching of the bow. Similarly I should accept the inter-pretation rejected by Wickham of

'sunt quibus in satura uidear nimis acer et ultra
legem tendere opus; sine neruis altera quidquid
conposui pars esse putat.

Horace, *Satires* 2 1 1-3

There are some people to whom I appear to be too sharp in my satire and to stretch my work further than the law allows; others believe that what I write is nerveless.

Better to translate the last clause 'that my bow doesn't have a string in it' rather than deny that *acer* speaks to *tendere*[10] and *neruis* to both of them, and better to talk of ridicule cutting sharper than anger than to trans-late

ridiculum acri
fortius ac melius magnas plerumque secat res.

Horace *Satires* 1 10 14-5

without suggesting that *acri* speaks to *secat*. But this is what usually happens, as for instance in the most recent trans-lation, 'Great issues are usually resolved more forcefully and effectively by wit than by castigation'.

Of course there are such things as mortified metaphors, even in Latin. Nevertheless, in the present state of our understanding of Lucretius, there is little harm done if for a change somebody calls the dead to life. It is better to see a little too much than not to see anything.

So our consideration of these last few passages has shown that Lucretius is capable of running two images together. But often the texture of the poetry seems to be even more complex, shot through with swift glimpses of things which greatly enrich its effect:

Vast images in glimmering dawn
Half shown are broken and withdrawn.
Tennyson

Surely something can be done about these unidentifiable objects. It is defeatism to classify Lucretius 1 62-79 as Townend 107 appears to do as a 'pure metaphor', 'with imagery derived from no clearly identifiable source, and suggesting visions altogether of the mind'.[11]

6. Building and Similes

'Rough weary roads through barren wilds he tried
yet still he marches with true Roman pride.'
J. Armstrong

*Tornus, trocleas et tympana, rotas atque austra, regula . . .
normaque . . . et libella, insilia ac fusi radii scapique sonantes,
materiemque dolare ac leuia radere tigna et terebrare etiam
ac pertundere perque forare,* the lathe, pulleys and tread-
wheels, water wheels and scooping pans, the rule, the square
and the lead, heddles and spindles, shuttles and banging
yard-beams, the axe and the plane, the gimlet too and the
punch and the bradawl – there is a fearful clatter of tools in
the *De Rerum Natura.* This chapter will examine a few
images drawn from building and from these will move to an
analysis of the technique of some of Lucretius' similes.
¶ *The Toppling Building.* If you believe that in the past
the world suffered drought earthquake and flood, you must
believe also that it is liable to be destroyed in the
future:

> nam cum res tantis morbis tantisque periclis
> temptarentur, ibi si tristior incubuisset
> causa, darent late cladem magnasque ruinas.
>
> 5 345-7
>
> *Since it was subject to these ailments and perils, if some more
> powerful agent had added its weight it would have fallen in
> a great wide ruin.*

If something leans on something else (*incubuisset* 346) and
produces a great wide ruin, we are made to see a tall tree or
a building swaying and toppling so that pressure on the side
of it is enough to knock it down. This is a common enough
metaphor seen at its simplest in Plautus *Aulularia* 594 *quo*

incumbat eo impellere, and less sharply in the appeal directed
by Aeneas to his father Anchises:

> . . . ne uertere secum
> cuncta pater fatoque urguenti incumbere uellet.
> abnegat inceptoque et sedibus haeret in isdem.

Aeneid 2 652 - 4

*. . . not to bring down everything in his own ruin, not to add
his weight to the pressure of fate. He refused and stuck to his
resolution and stayed where he was.*

If Anchises stays in Troy, it will be the end of everything.
He will be leaning on Fate which is already pressing.

¶ *The Fall and the Fire.* If the outlines are vague in the
last citation from Lucretius, there is little doubt about the
rickety house in the atomic explanation of hunger and eat -
ing, thirst and drinking:

> his igitur rebus rarescit corpus et omnis
> subruitur natura, dolor quam consequitur rem.
> propterea capitur cibus, ut suffulciat artus
> et recreet uires inter datus, atque patentem
> per membra ac uenas ut amorem opturet edendi.
> umor item discedit in omnia quae loca cumque   870
> poscunt umorem; glomerataque multa uaporis
> corpora, quae stomacho praebent incendia nostro,
> dissupat adueniens liquor ac restinguit ut ignem,
> urere ne possit calor amplius aridus artus,
> sic igitur tibi anhela sitis de corpore nostro   875
> abluitur, sic expletur ieiuna cupido.

4 865 - 876

*As a result of this, the body grows less compact and is
completely undermined; this is followed by pain. For this
reason we take food to prop up our limbs to fill up the spaces
and restore our strength, and throughout our limbs and veins
to stop up the gaping desire to eat. In the same way fluid is
distributed amongst whatever parts of the body require it and
the great numbers of heat particles which set fire to our*

stomach are scattered by the arrival of the liquid and quenched
like a fire, so that the dry heat can no longer scorch our limbs.
So now you know how the gasping thirst is leached out of the
body, and how your hunger is filled.

Here we have two clear metaphors. When a building is
being undermined (*subruitur*), cracks develop in its fabric
(*rarescit*). We then have to shore up parts of it (*suffulciat*)
and strengthen it internally (*inter datus*), and close up the
fissures (*patentem opturet*). Except the undermining all this
fits the atomic explanation of hunger and eating quite
directly. The body is not undermined when we grow hungry,
in the sense that the ground we walk on remains unmoved.
Surely Lucretius means that the rarefaction of hunger
weakens the body internally, that it bores under the skin.
This metaphor is absolutely obvious and vivid and yet
when the translators come to *expletur*, the conclusion of the
argument, they offer 'satisfied' 'appeased' 'glutted', even
'se dissipe' and 'gestillt'. Rouse is best with 'fulfilled', but
he seems to misunderstand the passage by saying in his
note that all its metaphors are drawn from a building set on
fire.

But Lucretius does not conflate the two metaphors. The
fire is separate from the building, as hunger is different
from thirst. When we are thirsty many heat particles gather
in our stomach and set a fire going. When water arrives
it damps down the heat, it puts out the fire. Lines
875-6 state the two separate conclusions, that this is
how thirst is washed out of the body, and how hunger
is filled up.

¶ *A Demolition.* 'The impious man is not the one who
denies the gods of the vulgar, but the one who attaches the
opinion of the vulgar to the gods' (Epicurus in Diogenes
Laertius 10 123). A resounding demolition occurs when
Lucretius is attacking the vulgar opinion that the gods
created the world:

dicere porro hominum causa uoluisse parare
praeclaram mundi naturam proptereaque
adlaudabile opus diuom laudare decere
aeternumque putare atque inmortale futurum,
nec fas esse, deum quod sit ratione uetusta   160
gentibus humanis fundatum perpetuo aeuo,
sollicitare suis ulla ui ex sedibus umquam
nec uerbis uexare et ab imo euertere summa,
cetera de genere hoc adfingere et addere, Memmi,
desiperest.

5 156 - 65

*To go on to say that for the sake of mankind the gods took
it into their heads to create this excellent world and for this
reason that it becomes us to praise the praiseworthy work of
the gods and believe that it is going to be everlasting and
immortal and that since the gods have built it up by ancient
design to benefit humanity for all time, it would be impious
ever to bring any force to bear on it or to shake it from its
foundations or to jolt it with words or turn it upside down,
all this mass of fantasy, Memmius, is absolute nonsense.*

The tone of this passage is derisive. Lucretius does not
agree that the world is excellent; on the contrary he is just
about to expatiate on its shortcomings and discomforts
(5 198 - 221). But to catch the full flavour of the contempt one
must read the passage aloud. The ironic reference to the
excellence of the world is conveyed in a jingle *parare
praeclaram*, followed immediately in case we miss it by a
withering *figura etymologica* in *adlaudabile laudare,* and now
that our ears are attuned to the long *a* carrying the word
accent and the verse ictus, we hear the disdain in *putare
atque immortale.* In 162 - 3 the rush of nine sibilants in two
lines is not idle, and a last contemptuous assonance routs
the pious – and the translators – in *adfingere et addere.* By
this 'fabric of fabrications' Lucretius means the great
edifice of ten infinitive verbs in the eight lines that precede.

The terms which refer to a building and its demolition are in lines 161-3; *fundatum*, frequently used in such meta - phors in Lucretius (we are about to study an example in 4 506), also *sollicitare ex sedibus* (compare 6 574), and *uexare* (compare 5 340).

On *ab imo euertere summa* the best comment is again in Virgil, in the second line of the passage where Aeneas is describing what he saw from the roof of Priam's palace:

tum uero omne mihi uisum considere in ignis
Ilium et ex imo uerti Neptunia Troia,   625
ac ueluti summis antiquam in montibus ornum
cum ferro accisam crebrisque bipennibus instant
eruere agricolae certatim, illa usque minatur
et tremefacta comam concusso uertice nutat,
uolneribus donec paulatim euicta supremum   630
congemuit traxitque iugis auolsa ruinam.

   Aeneid 2 624-31

Then I saw the whole of Ilium settling down into the flames and Neptune's Troy turning over from its foundations; just as when the trunk of an ancient ash on the mountain top has been hacked by the steel and the countrymen strive to fell it with quickly alternating axe-blows and it keeps teetering, and its hair trembles and it nods its shuddering head until, gradually overcome by its wounds, it gives a last cry, breaks and spreads destruction on the ridge.

The essential almost explicit resemblance between the buildings of Troy and the mountain ash is that both are falling in the same way with their tops curving down in a quarter circle. *Ex imo uerti*, to turn from the bottom, is caught up and developed by the mention of the shuddering head and the lateral havoc. It is because of this vivid realiza - tion of the meaning of *ex imo uerti*, that this passage in the *Aeneid* has been quoted. But it is only fair to say that this essential resemblance has no place in the standard English commentary by Austin, and that the Penguin translation

by Jackson Knight has nearly a dozen mistakes in these
eight lines:

*And in truth all Ilium was now, visibly before me, settling
into the fires, and Neptune's own Troy, uprooted, was
overturning; like an ancient rowan-tree high up among
the mountains, which, hacked with stroke after stroke of iron
axes by farmers vying all round to dislodge it, begins to
tremble and continues threatening while the crest shakes and
the high boughs sway, till gradually vanquished it gives a
final groan and at last overcome by the wounds and wrenched
from its place it trails havoc down the mountain-side.*

This does show once again the dangers of reading the classics
in translation. In certain circumstances we have to do this,
but it is not reading the classics.

¶ *Off the true.* The most elaborate building image in Lucretius
occurs in the following simile. Lucretius complained in his
preface about the poverty of the Latin language, but if
the Epicurean philosopher in his Garden was embarrassed
by this, it certainly doesn't appear to have hampered the
joiner on the building site:

denique ut in fabrica, si prauast regula prima,
normaque si fallax rectis regionibus exit,
et libella aliqua si ex parti claudicat hilum,   515
omnia mendose fieri atque obstipa necessu est
praua cubantia prona supina atque absona tecta,
iam ruere ut quaedam uideantur uelle, ruantque
prodita iudiciis fallacibus omnia primis,
sic igitur ratio tibi rerum praua necessest   520
falsaque sit, falsis quae cumque ab sensibus ortast.

4 513-21

*Finally as in a building if the original ruler is not straight,
if the square is not true but deviates from the right angle, if
the plumb line wavers at all in any direction, the whole
house must go wrong and leave the vertical, crooked and
bulging, leaning forward leaning back and not fitting*

*properly, so that parts of it seem to be wanting to fall
instantly, and that all of it would fall, betrayed by the
original judgments which <u>were not true</u>. So therefore
whatever reasoning you may do about the world, it could not
be <u>straight</u> and <u>truthful</u>, if it is erected upon senses which
are <u>not truthful</u>.*

The close fit of simile and illustrandum is pointed by the
repetition of *praua*, the play between *fallax fallacibus
falsaque falsis*, and the reminiscence in the last word *ortast*
of the simile that has preceded.

All this is clear in the Latin if not in the translations, but
there is more to it than this. There are two illuminating
questions we can ask about this crooked house. First, why
does Lucretius refer to a first ruler, *regula prima*? Is this
the ruler the surveyor started out with? Perhaps, but it
remains a surprising expression. Second, why does Lucretius
in lines 518-9 distinguish between parts of the building and
the whole of it? To say that parts seem to be wanting to
fall immediately and that the whole building would fall
makes an interesting distinction, but there is more to it
than that. The answers to these questions are to be found
in the context in which the simile occurs:

> . . . praestat rationis egentem
> reddere mendose causas utriusque figurae,
> quam manibus manifesta suis emittere quoquam
> et uiolare fidem primam et conuellere tota   505
> fundamenta quibus nixatur uita salusque.
> non modo enim ratio ruat omnis, uita quoque ipsa
> concidat extemplo, nisi credere sensibus ausis
> praecipitisque locos uitare et cetera quae sint
> in genere hoc fugienda, sequi contraria quae sint.   510
>   4 502-10

*. . . it is better for a man who does not know the reason to
give wrong explanations than to let the obvious slip out of his
fingers, to go against the primary evidence, to tear up all the*

*foundations on which our lives and our safety rest. For not
only the whole of your reasoning would fall, but life itself
would collapse in an instant, if you were not to have the
courage to believe your senses, and to avoid steep places
and everything of this sort which must be avoided and to
follow the opposite.*

Our first question is answered in line 505; the senses are
our *fides prima*, our primary evidence, and when we reach
regula prima in the simile we see that we are not to worry
too much about the first ruler on a building project. It is in
the simile in order to pick up the *fides prima* in the literal
argument. Our second question is also answered in advance.
In 507ff. we read that if you were not to believe in the senses
not only would the whole of your reasoning fall but life
itself would fall instantly because you would not be able
to walk safely. So in 517ff. we are told that in a building
whose original ruler is not straight some parts of it would
seem to wish to fall immediately and the whole building
would fall betrayed by its false primary judgments. The
parts which wish to fall immediately (*iam ruere*) clearly
correspond to life itself (*concidat extemplo*); the whole
building (*ruantque omnia*) refers to the whole of their
reasoning (*ratio ruat omnis*), and the false primary judgments in 519 represent the discredited senses in 508, which
have just been called the primary evidence in 505.

This shows how far Lucretius is willing to go in his deter-
mination to point the resemblances between simile and
illustrandum. And it is not simply a question of verbal
correspondences. Lucretius is perfectly willing to adjust
the details of the simile making them less natural and less
plausible as we see here with *regula prima*, and the parts of
the falling building. The very correspondences may be
fraudulent. There is something not quite fair in comparing
the parts and the whole of a building, with life and the
whole of the sceptic's reasoning. Further it needs all

Lucretius' verbal skill to conceal another discrepancy. In 518-9 parts of a building seem to want to fall before the whole of it, whereas in 507-8 life itself cannot properly be said to fall before the whole of the sceptic's reasoning. Lucretius has lulled our intelligence into accepting all this by his use of verbal echoes, and such is the impetus of the poetry and the polemic that all our logical discomforts are swept aside. ¶ *The Road to the Truth.* The sceptic who rejects the evidence of his senses we have just seen walking over a cliff. This was not strictly an image but a literal statement, but the notion that philosophy is a journey towards the truth is a not uncommon metaphor in Lucretius. We are also told how Epicurus pointed out the way by which we could hasten to the supreme Good by a short run on a straight path:

uiam monstrauit, tramite paruo
qua possemus ad id recto contendere cursu.
6 27-8

Again, instead of saying that the sense of touch is the most convincing form of evidence, he says that it is the shortest well-built road of belief into the breast of man, the site of his intelligence[12]:

uia qua munita fidei
proxima fert humanum in pectus templaque mentis.
5 102-3

It is less easy to see the road in the following passage but it is just as important not to lose it. Heracleitus and his followers are attacked

quia multa sibi cernunt contraria Musae
et fugitant in rebus inane relinquere purum,
ardua dum metuunt, amittunt uera uiae.
1 657-9

Because the Muses (i.e. Heracleitus and his followers) see many obstacles before them and shrink from positing the existence of pure void in objects, while they avoid the steep places they lose the true path.

Whether one thinks of hill-walking, which Lucretius seems to have enjoyed (4 575-9, 6 469), or road-building, for which the Romans are famous, the pictures are very useful to Lucretius' purpose, so useful, and so typical of the author that it may well be relevant to a textual problem. *Musae* is the nearest to what the manuscripts offer in line 657 (musę O mu QG). In Plato *Sophist* 242D the Stranger is making fun of the myths of early philosophers and refers to 'Ionian and later some Sicilian Muses, Ἰάδες καὶ Σικελαί τινες ὕστερον Μοῦσαι,' meaning the Ionian Heracleitus and his Sicilian followers including Empedocles. So in Lucretius *Musae* could refer to Heracleitus and his followers, perhaps including the Stoics. It is normal practice for ancient philosophers to coin nicknames for their opponents. Epicurus called Nausiphanes the Jelly-fish, Plato the Golden Man and his followers the Flatterers of Dionysos (Diogenes Laertius 10 8). And it would be just like Lucretius to mimic the oracular obscurity of Heracleitus while condemning this overrated philosopher whose dark sayings had won him such a bright reputation (*clarus ob obscuram linguam* 1 639). For instance many scholars have found a pun just before our passage, *stolidi* in line 641 suggesting *Stoici*, although this was before Furley's recent demonstration that there is no need to believe that Lucretius attacks the Stoics.

To return to the image. There can be no doubt about the correlation of *ardua* and *uiai* in line 659. This traveller who hasn't the courage to go straight over the hill like any normal Roman road but twists about in detours to avoid the climb, this is so Lucretian that one is strongly inclined to keep *contraria* in line 657 in the same image, 'the obstacles in their path'. About half the conjectures which have been put forward to take the place of *Musae* do not fit the image very well, and the interpretation of Pascal and Müller 119, 'because they see many things which are each other's opposites', does not fit it at all. If then we argue that this image may well be active in *contraria*, then we *may* well have a new point in *Musae* and a new justification of that reading. The natural habitat of the Muses is on the high peaks. If they are jibbing at obstacles and avoiding their natural habitat, they are certainly losing their way.

This is the most that can be done for *Musae*, and this interpretation is offered here in the belief that the scholar tackling a difficult passage should first do his best for what the manuscripts seem to offer. This is the necessary ground-work, and it had not yet been done for this passage. But *Musae* remains such an impenetrably obscure way of referring to the Heracleiteans, that it must be held to be a corrupt reading.

¶ *Similes*. These interpretations would not be convincing unless it could be shown that Lucretius often engineers his similes to fit closely into their contexts. This is so easy that it will be enough to refer to 1 271-94 and 936-47 with Parker's treatment of them, and to examine here just one simile from this point of view:

uerum animo satis haec uestigia parua sagaci
sunt per quae possis cognoscere cetera tute.
namque canes ut montiuagae persaepe ferai
naribus inueniunt intectas fronde quietes,   405
cum semel institerunt uestigia certa uiai,
sic alid ex alio per te tute ipse uidere
talibus in rebus poteris caecasque latebras
insinuare omnis et uerum protrahere inde.
quod si pigraris paulumue recesseris ab re. . .   410
      1 402-10

But these tiny tracks are enough to enable your keen-scented mind to recognize everything else. For just as dogs often smell out the refuge of a mountain beast hidden in the undergrowth, if once they start upon the right tracks, so too

*will you be able to find out for yourself one thing from the
other in these matters and penetrate all the unseen lairs and
drag the truth out of them. But if you are slow or hang back
a little . . .*

Here we find many of the phenomena we have just noted
in the building simile. The verbal parallelisms are close,
between *uestigia parua* and *uestigia certa, sagaci* and *naribus,
per quae cetera* and *alid ex alio, cognoscere* and *uidere, tute*
and *tute, intectas quietes* and *caecas latebras*. Apart from these
explicit correspondences or repetitions, the context contains
hunting words which have no parallel in the simile, because
none is needed. The imagination of the reader is already so
charged that he is compelled to see the hunting application
of lines 409 and 410. The dog, that is the pupil, has found an
animal lair in the undergrowth. In 409, if the pupil is
zealous, he works his way through the tangle and drags
out the quarry; in 410 if he is indolent or spiritless, he hangs
back and won't go in after it. The transfusion of terms
discussed in chapter four occurs with all these hunting
terms which are not in the simile but it is less conspicuous
here because they fit the context perfectly smoothly and
comprehensibly.

The intimate correspondence between simile and context will be further studied in the example which opens
chapter eight. Here we shall look at a passage which is not
a simile but which demonstrates how this technique can be
at work where there is no simile.

Lucretius is arguing that the multitude of diseases which
attack the body and the variety of shocks which assault the
world are both easily explained in view of the infinite
number of different atoms streaming in from the infinite
universe upon our infinitesimal world:

numquis enim nostrum miratur, siquis in artus
accepit calido febrim feruore coortam
aut alium quemuis morbi per membra dolorem?

opturgescit enim subito pes, arripit acer
saepe dolor dentes, oculos inuadit in ipsos,
existit sacer ignis et urit corpore serpens   660
quam cumque arripuit partem repitque per artus,
ni mirum, quia sunt multarum semina rerum,
et satis haec tellus morbi caelumque mali fert,
unde queat uis immensi procrescere morbi.
    sic igitur toti caelo terraeque putandumst   665
ex infinito satis omnia suppeditare,
unde repente queat tellus concussa moueri
perque mare ac terras rapidus percurrere turbo,
ignis abundare Aetnaeus, flammescere caelum;
id quoque enim fit et ardescunt caelestia templa   670
et tempestates pluuiae grauiore coortu
sunt, ubi forte ita se tetulerunt semina aquarum.
    6 655-672

None of us is surprised if a man takes into his body a
fever which has gathered with burning heat, or any other
painful bodily affliction. For the foot suddenly swells up;
often a sharp pain seizes on the teeth, and forces an entry
right into the eyes; the cursed fire (of erysipelas or shingles)
starts up and creeps over the body burning whatever part
it seizes upon and crawls over the limbs: surely because there
are seeds of many things and this earth and sky produce
malignant disease in sufficient quantity to beget an im-
measurable progeny of disease.

    And this is how we must suppose that everything is
supplied in sufficient numbers from the infinite to the
whole of the sky and the earth to cause the land to be
suddenly struck and shaken, and to enable the rapacious
whirlwind to run all over sea and land, and the fire of Aetna
to overflow and the sky to flame. For that too happens and
the regions of the sky flash with lightning, and unusually
heavy rainstorms gather, when the seeds of water happen so to
move.

Diseases and storms are traced to the same atomic process, and it is typical of Lucretius that the medical and
meteorological terminology should be similar. In 662-4 the
sky and the earth produce enough ills and disease to be
able to beget an immeasurable progeny of disease (*satis . . .
tellus morbi caelumque . . . unde queat . . . immensi . . .
morbi*). So therefore in 665-7 for the whole earth and sky
everything is supplied in sufficient numbers from the infinite to be able to beget meteorological disturbances (*toti
caelo terraeque . . . ex infinito . . . satis omnia . . . unde . . .
queat*); the foot swells so the fires of Aetna abound (*obtur-
gescit . . . abundare*); toothache and erysipelas both seize
the parts affected, so the whirlwind snatches up everything
that lies in its path (*arripit . . . arripuit . . . rapidus*);
erysipelas crawls over the limbs, so the whirlwind runs
over the earth and sea (*repit per artus, per mare ac terras . . .
percurrere*); even the rhythm of the sentences in similar,
existit sacer ignis et urit corpore serpens 660, *ignis abundare
Aetnaeus, flammescere caelum* 669. After all those correspondences between pain and fire we must note that fever
and storm are both said to 'arise' (*coortam* 656 *coortu* 671),
and that in the last line the seeds of water are said to bear
themselves, just as in 662-3 it is suggested that the seeds of
many things are borne by the earth (*fert . . . tetulerunt*).
Why then does the foot swell suddenly when suddenness is
not a normal characteristic of attacks of gout? Can this
suddenness be there to provide a correlative to the suddenness of the earthquake (*subito* 658, *repente* 667)? Why is the
rain added after the two fires, Etna with its reflection in
the sky in 669 and then the lightning in 670? Can this
concentration of rain be there to provide a correlative to the
concentration of fluid in the gouty foot?

This is certainly how many similes work in Virgil as well
as in Lucretius. The poets cook both sets of data, slightly,
to make them look as like each other as possible. Here, for

instance, at least two of the correspondences are verbal rather than substantive. An *immeasurable* progeny of disease is set against the supply of everything from the *infinite;* the seeds of many things seem to be *borne* by the earth, and this is set against the gathering of rainstorms wherever the seeds of water chance to *bear* themselves.

One brief simile will confirm both of these points, the detailed verbal correspondences between simile and con-text, and the fraudulency of some of these correspondences:

praeterea cum rarescunt quoque nubila uentis
aut dissoluuntur solis super icta calore,
mittunt umorem pluuium stillantque, quasi igni
cera super calido tabescens multa liquescat.

6 513-6

Besides when too the clouds are thinned out by wind or loosened when they are struck from above by the heat of the sun, they exude rainy moisture and it drips just as wax melts and runs freely when it is above a hot fire.

This is a close analogy, and Lucretius emphasizes its closeness by verbal parallelisms: clouds drip *super icta calore*, just as wax melts *igni super calido. Calore* speaks to *calido*, and *super* is repeated. Fraudulently. For the clouds are struck from above, and the wax is above a fire.

7. Light and Fire and Fluidity of Imagery

¶ *Swift Lights*. Lights and fires terrestrial and celestial are the subject of this chapter and Lucretius is full of them. First we shall refer to a few brief passages where such images are fleetingly touched upon, but this chapter, like the three which precede it, will be attempting to isolate a general principle which Lucretius followed in organizing his images, in this case his habit of recurring again and again in an ex- tended passage to a dominant image; and most of the examples of images of fire and light will be chosen to enable us to examine this habit which I call fluidity of imagery.

Heracleitus we have met in the last chapter 'illustrious for his dark speech' *clarus ob obscuram linguam* (1 639); Memmius is called upon to listen clearly to these obscure arguments, *clarius audi. nec me animi fallit quam sint obscura* (1 921-2); on this dark theme Lucretius is com- posing luminous poetry, *obscura de re tam lucida pango carmina* (1 933-4); Epicurus is praised for taking human life out of great storm waves and great darkness and settling it in such a calm and in such a clear light:

fluctibus e tantis uitam tantisque tenebris

in tam tranquillo et tam clara luce locauit.

5 11-12

The symmetry of the language keeps separate the waves and the darkness, the calm and the light, but the frequency of hendiadys in Latin poetry (e.g. 5 1242) justifies the reader in running two things into one and seeing a dark storm followed by a still and sunlit sea. Epicurus, finally, according

to all the printed editions I have seen apart from Wakefield's, is praised, in the proem to Book 3, 'for first being
able to lift up such a clear light from such great darkness . . .'

e tenebris tantis tam clarum extollere lumen
qui primus potuisti . . .

But Timpanaro has shown that the reading in the archetype is *o tenebris tantis*, and that this reading is linguistically
unobjectionable. What he does not say is that the reading
of the archetype makes a splendid picture, 'O Epicurus,
who first were able to lift up such a clear light *amid* such
great darkness . . .' whereas the emendation accepted by
the editors does not quite make sense. If you lift up a light
from the darkness, what was it doing there? How would the
darkness have been dark if it were there? And where are
you holding it now? The preposition is not worthy of the
precise and vivid imagination of this poet.[13 ·]

These images are short and simple, but we shall now look
at light and fire images of somewhat larger compass and
try to indicate some of the complexities of their use.

¶ *Light and Looms*

nec me animi fallit Graiorum obscura reperta
difficile inlustrare Latinis uersibus esse,
multa nouis uerbis praesertim cum sit agendum
propter egestatem linguae et rerum nouitatem;
sed tua me uirtus tamen et sperata uoluptas   140
suauis amicitiae quemuis efferre laborem
suadet et inducit noctes uigilare serenas
quaerentem dictis quibus et quo carmine demum
clara tuae possim praepandere lumina menti,
res quibus occultas penitus conuisere possis.   145
hunc igitur terrorem animi tenebrasque necessest
non radii solis neque lucida tela diei
discutiant, sed naturae species ratioque,
principium cuius hinc nobis exordia sumet . . .

1 136-49

*Nor do I fail to realize that it is difficult to illumine the dark
discoveries of the Greeks in Latin verses particularly since
I have to work a great deal with new terms because of the
poverty of the language and novelty of the subject matter.
But for all that I am persuaded by your goodness and the
delightful prospect of the pleasure of your friendship to
endure any labour and to stay awake these clear nights
looking for the words and the poetry to open up at last
before your mind bright lights by which you may be able
to see to the very depths of hidden things. So therefore this
terror and darkness of the mind must be dispelled not by the
rays of the sun nor the bright shafts of daylight but by the
sight of Nature and the reason of it, and we shall make a
start in it from this point . . .*

This is basically the familiar antithesis between the
light of poetry and the darkness of philosophy. But it is
not all one light and one darkness. Metaphor apart, *noctes
uigilare serenas* is the phrase of a man who enjoyed the
solitude and serenity of working at night, and who couldn't
keep away from the window. In the first line of the extract
philosophy is dark but in 144 Lucretius is opening up light
before the mind of Memmius. *Penitus conuisere* (145) to see
to the heart, suggests that the Epicurean vision is not of the
superficies but of the inner atomic constitution of everything
in the Universe. In 146 darkness of mind is linked not as
before with philosophy, but with the fear of the after life,
and the reader's antennae are vibrated not only by this
switch in the application of the image but also perhaps by
a strange new image within the image. In weaving, *radii*
are shuttles as at 5 1353; *tela* (feminine singular as opposed
to *tela* neuter plural 'shafts') is the loom as at 5 1351, or
what is woven upon it, or strictly the vertical threads
through which the *radii* fly; and *exordium* is literally the
same as the last definition of *tela*. It's not the shuttles of the
sun or the warp of daylight that can dispel this dark fear, but

the warp of our poetry which I am just about to set up. This reaction is not as far-fetched as it may seem, and can be supported by passages where these metaphors are clearly alive and felt. *Exordium* or *exordiri* is not often used with a trace of its technical meaning, but such a use in Plautus, Cicero and Quintilian, is recorded in the Latin dictionaries. Similarly Plautus and Cicero show the metaphorical use of *tela*. Both occur together in

neque exordiri primum unde occipias habes
neque ad detexundam telam certos terminos.

  Plautus *Pseudolus* 399-400

*You haven't any point at which you must start your warp
nor a fixed point at which to cast off.*[14]

radii strictly are rods or staves, but the word is often used of the different sorts of radiating lines, the spokes of wheels, the radii of a halo or nimbus round a head, the rays of the sun. What makes the weaving reference here more likely is the Lucretian description of evaporation, *radiisque retexens aetherius sol* 5 267, 389, the sun unweaving the sea with the shuttles of its rays. Not that such a translation is possible. But the idea is in the Latin. If one had to unweave a piece and save the thread, one would presumably do it with the shuttle, opening the warp and sending the shuttle repeatedly back through it.

  This passage therefore has a light image in 136-7, a literal mention of light in 142, a light image with a different reference in 144-5, and another with yet another reference in 146-7, and in this last perhaps the vestige of another image within the light image. This fluidity of imagery is not an isolated phenomenon in Lucretius.

  ¶ *Light and Little Boys.* A similar irrational poetic disturbance is set up in another passage where light provides the main imagery. We start in a battle scene. Superstition, he is arguing, does not take fright and run away, *timefactae effugiunt*, from military power and paraphernalia, from

good breeding or from wealth; so when he goes on to refer
to superstitious fears and anxieties as *sequaces*, he is
making quite clear who the pursuer is and who the pursued.
This is foozled in the dogging and haunting and quälenden
and obsédants of the translators:

> quod si ridicula haec ludibriaque esse uidemus,
> re ueraque metus hominum curaeque sequaces
> nec metuunt sonitus armorum nec fera tela
> audacterque inter reges rerumque potentis   50
> uersantur neque fulgorem reuerentur ab auro
> nec clarum uestis splendorem purpureai,
> quid dubitas quin omnis sit haec rationis potestas,
> omnis cum in tenebris praesertim uita laboret?
> nam uel uti pueri trepidant atque omnia caecis   55
> in tenebris metuunt, sic nos in luce timemus
> inter dum, nihilo quae sunt metuenda magis quam
> quae pueri in tenebris pauitant finguntque futura.
>
> hunc igitur terrorem animi tenebrasque necessest
> non radii solis neque lucida tela diei   60
> discutiant, sed naturae species ratioque.

2 47-61

*But if we see that this is all contemptible and laughable and
if in actual fact the pursuing fears and anxieties of men are
undaunted by offensive weapons and the clash of arms and
boldly mix with kings and leaders of men and are no
respecters of the glow of gold or of the shining brilliance of
purple robes, why do you doubt that this is wholly within the
province of reason, particularly since our whole life labours
in darkness? For like frightened boys who are afraid of
everything because they can't see in the dark so do we sometimes in the light fear what is no more frightening than
what boys panic about in the dark and think is going to
happen. Therefore this darkness and terror of mind must be
dispelled not by the rays of the sun nor the bright shafts of
daylight, but by the sight of Nature and reason of it.*

At the beginning fear is contrasted with martial panoply and wordly power and Lucretius expresses this contrast in terms of light, the glow of gold, and the shining brilliance of purple robes. Despite these dazzling appurtenances our life is spent in darkness. To justify this claim Lucretius argues that although we live in daylight, we behave like little boys in the darkness. That is, we are afraid of coats hanging on the back of doors and of a wide range of monsters likely to come and get us. In *quae pueri pauitant finguntque futura* these two aspects are carefully separated, the fear of what is and the illusion of what is coming. This is poetry for its suggestion of the emotions of the child's bedroom. But since we have already noted how closely the details of Lucretius' similes can fit their contexts, we must ask here if the distinction between the child's present fears and future imaginings has any analogue in the surrounding context. Surely it lies in the distinction between the *religiones* and *mortis timores* in 44-5. Lucretius is neatly suggesting the puerility of our fears not only in this world but also for the next. Yet again this vital poetic distinction is smoothed away by some of the translators, 'those horrors which children imagine coming upon them in the dark'. At the end we revert to the three weaving lines we have already discussed but in this repetition they take on a new force from their context. In 1 146-8 the shuttles of the sun were unable to dispel the darkness of fear and the reader saw them in contrast with the light of philosophy; whereas now in the second book they are seen against the flashiness of power and wealth and the darkness in a child's bedroom.

In view of his famous statement about the inadequacy of the Latin language for the exposition of Epicurean philosophy (1 139), it is tempting here to point to the characteristic opulence of Lucretius' vocabulary. In line 56 *metuenda* picks up *metuunt* deliberately to provide a logical signpost between simile and illustrandum, but the translator soon notices that Lucretius has four other 'fear' words in these five lines. Similarly this whole play with the darkness of our lives, the inadequacy of the wordly lights, and the light of Epicurean philosophy, runs through the whole of the introduction to this book and the 'light' vocabulary is inexhaustible, *templa serena, pectora caeca, aurea simulacra, lampadas igniferas, lumina nocturnis epulis, argento fulget, laqueata aurataque templa, auro renidet* answered by *tempestas adridet.*

This use of the same image in different relationships throughout a large context, is what I am calling fluidity of imagery and I shall go on to trace it in several other passages in this chapter.

But in this passage there are other images hidden away amongst all this light. Wealth can lay a bed of luxury for a man (22); but Nature feels no lack if you lie out in the soft grass (29), sprinkled with flowers (33); you don't get rid of fever any quicker if you lie on purple or on embroidered coverlets (33-6), where surely *textilibus in picturis* answers *conspergunt uiridantibus floribus herbas*; and yet in this paragraph instead of laying a bed at *substernere* in line 22, the bowdlerizers translate 'supply', 'minister to us', 'bieten', and even 'lui procurer maint plaisir'. Characteristic too of the sensuous prodigality of this poet is the sudden intrusion of acoustical phenomena when the arms clash in 49 in the middle of all this visualization.

I am sorry to keep harping on about translators' failures. This is not just scholar's jaundice. These are translations by the best Lucretian scholars and I am exposing their betrayal of the imagery in order to show that although most of what I write in this book is obvious, it is not unnecessary to write it. In reading poetry we are not cruising along an embanked autobahn, but rather exploring a hill track. We should go slowly and look at the view.

¶ *Fire Fanned into Flame.* The dividing line between fire and light is easily crossed in Lucretius. We too shall cross it in finding another example of fluidity of imagery:

numquam Tyndaridis forma conflatus amoris
ignis Alexandri Phrygio sub pectore gliscens
clara accendisset saeui certamina belli,   475
nec clam durateus Troiianis Pergama partu
inflammasset equos nocturno Graiiugenarum.

1 473-77

Never would the fire of love smouldering deep in the Trojan heart of Paris have been fanned by the beauty of Tyndareus' daughter, and set ablaze the bright struggles of war nor would the wooden horse with its litter of Greeks emerging at night have tricked the Trojans and put their city to the flames.

In 473-4 the fire is love; in 475 it ignites the bright fire of war; in 477 it is literal flames. In passing we note the mimic at work again modulating his voice to his subject matter. An epic theme fills Lucretius with poetic afflatus. Helen is dignified by a resonant patronymic, the Phrygian heart of Alexander is a fine Epic synallage like the derisive Nemean maw of lion *Nemeaeus enim nobis nunc magnus hiatus ille leonis* (5 24-5) or the Thessalian colour of shell fish in the contemptuous display of Greek luxuries in

iam tibi barbaricae uestes Meliboeaque fulgens
purpura Thessalico concharum tacta colore

2 500-1

Durateus is a transliteration of the Homeric epithet, found only here in Latin, and the whole example is rounded off by the thunder of four words in one line, the last of them a Greek proper name with five syllables (cf. Virgil *Aeneid* 6 483 and Norden 438).

This very use of *conflare*, to fan into flames, recurs in 3 335-6, and very vividly in the account of the physiology of sleep:

nunc quibus ille modis somnus per membra quietem
inriget atque animi curas e pectore soluat,
suauidicis potius quam multis uersibus edam.
. . .
principio somnus fit ubi est distracta per artus
uis animae partimque foras eiecta recessit
et partim contrusa magis concessit in altum;
dissoluuntur enim tum demum membra fluuntque.
nam dubium non est, animai quin opera sit   920
sensus hic in nobis, quem cum sopor inpedit esse,
tum nobis animam perturbatam esse putandumst
eiectamque foras; non omnem, namque iaceret
aeterno corpus perfusum frigore leti.
quippe ubi nulla latens animai pars remaneret   925
in membris, cinere ut multa latet obrutus ignis,
unde reconflari sensus per membra repente
possit, ut ex igni caeco consurgere flamma?
    4 907-9, 916-28
*Now I shall expound in a few sweet spoken verses the ways
by which sleep infuses quiet over our limbs and melts the
cares of the mind out of the breast. . . . In the first place
sleep occurs when part of the spirit is dispersed throughout
the limbs, part of it is driven out and withdraws, and part
of it is thrust together and goes deeper into the body. That is
when the limbs are dissolved and fluid. For there is no
doubt that this consciousness of ours is the work of spirit,
and when sleep interferes with our consciousness, then we
must conclude that our spirit is disturbed and driven out of
the body: not in its entirety, since if it were, our body would
be submerged in the never ending chill of death. For if there
were no particle of spirit latent in our bodies like a latent
fire smouldering under heaps of ashes, whence could our
senses be suddenly fanned into flame again throughout our
bodies, as flame can rise from unseen fire?*

At the beginning sleep provides a douche of quiet, it melts the cares of the mind from the breast which is the seat of mind. This perhaps suggests a connection between cares and ice, which is thoroughly Lucretian, as in his description of the beginnings of love, which comes a few lines later:

hinc illaec primum Veneris dulcedinis in cor
stillauit gutta, et successit frigida cura.

4 1059-60

From here comes the first drip of the sweetness of Venus into our hearts. The chilling care comes later.

In our normal waking state our spirit is distributed throughout our bodies (3 231ff.). In sleep it is divided into three. Some of it is so thinned out throughout our bodies that it is too weak to set in motion the sensory processes (4 944-8). Some of it escapes from our body. Some of it withdraws deep into the body. The result of this is that the body relaxes, and this is expressed in line 919 in terms of the liquid image with which the paragraph started. Sleep pours its quiet over us, and our limbs are dissolved and flow. Not all of our spirit leaves the body. If it did, according to line 924 the body would lie soaked in the eternal cold of death. *Perfusum* saturated, suggests an excess of the liquid of sleep. And since this would result in death, Lucretius comes back to the notion of cold which has already been lightly suggested in line 908. This passage therefore provides another example of what I have called the fluidity of imagery – the use of one image in different functions in an extended context.

The simile with which the paragraph ends is again very precisely pointed. During sleep the third part of the spirit is *latens in membris* as fire *multa latet cinere ;* the fire is buried under a lot of ash, suggesting that the third part of the spirit withdraws deep into the body, as we have been told explicitly in 918. Flame rises from this unseen fire, so from the hidden third part of the spirit the action of the senses is fanned into flame in 927. This analysis is provided in order to show how Lucretius uses the simile as dialectical instrument, with separate details of the illustration each striking a blow for the argument. It also brings out the now familiar sleight of mind whereby Lucretius transfuses a term from the illustration into the illustrandum. In line 927 the senses should start up again, strictly they should not be fanned into flame. But by this point Lucretius has so established the analogy that we accept the metaphorical term. 'Rekindled' is the stock translation but it is not good enough. We must have a breath of air because that is an-other meaning of *anima*, and it is the return of *anima* from outside which reactivates the senses.

¶ *Light and Liquid*. Light is not only an important image, it is also an important topic on which to hang images. It is not only the view, it is also the road. To illustrate this we shall look at a few passages where the sun is referred to in liquid terms.

Lucretius had an eye and an ear for streams, and used his observations to produce great poetry, as in his evocation of the woodland habitat of primitive man:

... quibus e scibant umore fluenta
lubrica proluuie larga lauere umida saxa   950
umida saxa, super uiridi stillantia musco,
et partim plano scatere atque erumpere campo.
    5 949-52

Here Lucretius describes and the reader can hear three different water noises, as separated by my commas, and typically when the water drips in the third line, the auditory stimuli are suddenly enriched by all the visual and tactile effect of the green moss. We have seen that light is often used by Lucretius as an image for what is joyous, life-giving and truthful. In this section it joins the delight he takes in all the variety of river phenomena and the fusion of these two delights produces this unique poetry.

In 5 281-2 for example, the sun is a full fountain of
liquid light endlessly irrigating the sky:
  largus item liquidi fons luminis, aetherius sol
  inrigat adsidue caelum
and later in this book, where Lucretius is explaining how the
great immensity of light can be provided by the tiny disc of
the sun, the river language is very conspicuous:
  illud item non est mirandum, qua ratione
  tantulus ille queat tantum sol mittere lumen,
  quod maria ac terras omnis caelumque rigando
  compleat et calido perfundat cuncta uapore.   593
  nam licet hinc mundi patefactum totius unum   597
  largifluum fontem scatere atque erumpere lumen,
  ex omni mundo quia sic elementa uaporis
  undique conueniunt et sic coniectus eorum   600
  confluit, ex uno capite hic ut profluat ardor.
  nonne uides etiam quam late paruus aquai
  prata riget fons inter dum campisque redundet?
    5 590 - 603

Nor is there anything remarkable about that tiny sun shed-
ding such an immense light to bathe and fill all the lands
and seas and sky and to saturate everything in the warmth
of its heat. For it is quite possible for the one and only free-
flowing fountain of the whole world to emerge at this point
and spill over and send out its bursting light, because the
elements of heat come together in such a way from all sides
from the whole world, and flow together in such a con-
glomeration that this blazing heat flows out from this one
source. Don't you see how broadly a tiny spring too can
water the fields sometimes and spill over the plains.

This passage about light is saturated with liquid terms,
as can be seen immediately by reference to the two extracts
already quoted in this section. *Rigando* and *perfundat* in
592-3 are no doubt reinforced by *vapore* which means steam,
exhalation, as well as heat. All this river language gives the

poetry its impetus and joy, but apart from that it is fairly and squarely in the argument. In prosaic terms Lucretius' first explanation in 599-601 is that all heat from the earth rises and gathers at the sun and is then projected back at the earth. This is an endless cycle like the cycle of rivers – source, sea, clouds, source. ... The second argument in 602, is an analogical argument introduced as frequently by *nonne uides*, that a little spring can irrigate a broad plain therefore a little sun can fill the whole world. But in poetic terms the arguments are not so coldly distinguished and in characteristic Lucretian style, the first argument is expressed in metaphorical terms which anticipate and perhaps even weaken the analogy which follows.

All this is necessary to the understanding of Lucretius' proof that the speed of atoms is greater than the speed of light. His first point, in outline, is that light is without doubt ineffably fast, and yet is impeded by particles floating in the air, whereas the movement of atoms, being through the void, is wholly unimpeded and therefore faster:

nunc quae mobilitas sit reddita materiai
corporibus, paucis licet hinc cognoscere, Memmi.
primum aurora nouo cum spargit lumine terras
et uariae uolucres nemora auia peruolitantes   145
aera per tenerum liquidis loca uocibus opplent,
quam subito soleat sol ortus tempore tali
conuestire sua perfundens omnia luce,
omnibus in promptu manifestumque esse uidemus.
at uapor is, quem sol mittit, lumenque serenum   150
non per inane meat uacuum; quo tardius ire
cogitur, aerias quasi dum diuerberat undas.

  2 142-52

Now Memmius you will be able to see from my next few words what is the speed of atoms. First of all when the dawn sprinkles the earth with its new light, and the different birds

go flying through the trackless groves through the soft air,
filling everywhere with their liquid voices, it is perfectly
obvious to everyone how quickly the sun having arisen at
such a time clothes everything and soaks it in its light. But
the heat and bright light emitted by the sun do not go through
empty void; so it is compelled to slow down as it beats
through the waves of air.

Once again light is expressed in liquid terms. It is
sprinkled on the earth at dawn in 144, and soon after the
sun has risen it has soaked everything with light in 148.
But this liquid is not kept in a separate container, it leaks
all over the passage. The birds in line 146 fill the place with
their liquid voices. And just as their liquid voices go through
the soft air, the light shed by the sun beats through the
waves of air. The air too is liquid and, as Boyancé sees 296,
the slow and strenuous progress of the light through it is
likened in the word *diuerberat* to the strenuous effort of
swimming.[15] If something is beating through waves, there
is surely a suggestion of swimming. Nor is there anything odd
about waves of air. There is a great sea of air in 5 276 *aeris
magnum mare* in a different context, and winds are compared
to rivers in exuberant detail in 1 280 - 97. All in all Sand -
bach's objection to this image seems to be over - precise, and
his emendation unnecessary. It is wholly in Lucretius'
manner to use the same image three times in rapid succession
in different relationships.[16]

¶ *Imagery and Poetry.* In leaving these images I shall try
to assess the method I have followed. The simple procedure
has been to assert the literal sense of words used metaphoric -
ally. The two main dangers are that I have wasted every -
body's time by pointing out the obvious, and this is why I
have so often quoted the translators and commentators.
The literal force of the words may be obvious to readers of
Lucretius, but it does not seem to have reached those who
write about him. The second difficulty is that I may have

tried to inject life into metaphors that were dead for the poet and his contemporaries. This mistake is more likely to have been made with established metaphors. I am more likely to be wrong on *tendere oculos* on page 62 than on *nictantia fulgura* on page 8. It is also more likely with a single word, but if several metaphorical words in one context are coherent at a literal level, I have considered this as an indication of the life of the metaphor for the poet and his readers.[17] Those who reject these would argue that such words are not correlated, but are accidental juxtapositions of the same mortified metaphors. This Wickham would no doubt have argued with reference to *acer, tendere* and *neruis* on page 62, and anybody would be justified in feeling that it is a pure coincidence that *contraria* can refer to journeying on page 73 or that *radii, tela* and *exordia* have a weaving sense on page 81.

But even when the critic correctly understands the poet in exploring the details of the fit between image and illustrandum, he is the owl to the eagle. By the time he propounds his analyses of correspondences and discrepancies, of transfusion of terms and fluidity of imagery, categorizing and docketing, the poetry is no longer exciting. But there is no doubt that some part of its power lies in the associations. 'Only connect' is the legend on the title page of E. M. Forster's 'Howards End'. Lucretius was connecting all the time and if we are to read him justly, we must not miss the associations he is always seeing.

8. Religion and Word Play

'For every wise man has pure and holy opinions about the Divine and believes in its greatness and majesty. And particularly at festivals through having its name always on his lips he grasps the imperishable nature of the gods with intense emotion.' Epicurus

Most studies of Lucretius' imagery devote some attention to the use of Greek mythology for the purpose of allegory (for example, Sullwold 53-72 and Townend 99-100). Our own survey will end with a brief look at this topic to test the methods we have been evolving and show again how little the poetry is understood. A necessary preparation for this is a brief statement of the importance of word play in Lucretius, and a typical example is provided by the passage where he compares the act of love to a battle.

¶ *Puns.*

inritata tument loca semine fitque uoluntas
eicere id quo se contendit dira lubido,
idque petit corpus, mens unde est saucia amore;
namque omnes plerumque cadunt in uulnus et illam
emicat in partem sanguis, unde icimur ictu,   1050
et si comminus est, hostem ruber occupat umor.
sic igitur Veneris qui telis accipit ictus,
siue puer membris muliebribus hunc iaculatur
seu mulier toto iactans e corpore amorem,
unde feritur, eo tendit gestitque coire   1055
et iacere umorem in corpus de corpore ductum;
namque uoluptatem praesagit muta cupido.
    haec Venus est nobis; hinc autemst nomen Amoris,
hinc illaec primum Veneris dulcedinis in cor
stillauit gutta et successit frigida cura.
    4 1045-1060

These parts are stimulated and swell with seed and there arises a wish to eject it in the same direction as our fierce desires are marching, and the body makes for what has wounded the mind with love.

For men usually fall towards their wound and the blood spurts out in the direction from which comes the blow that strikes us, and in a close engagement the red fluid falls upon the enemy. So therefore the man who is wounded by the weapons of Venus whether he is being bombarded by a young boy with effeminate limbs, or whether it is a woman who is hurling love at him from her whole body, advances in the direction from which he is struck and longs to get to grips and to project the fluid from body to body, for his inarticulate desire anticipates some pleasure.

That's what our love is: This in fact is the origin of the name of love, this is the source of that drop of the sweetness of Venus which first trickles into our heart. The cold care comes later.

Sic igitur in 1052 informs us that the military picture that precedes is a simile. To reinforce our previous conclusion about the closeness of verbal correspondence between simile and context in Lucretius, we should note, *unde* picked up by *unde, icimur ictu* by *accipit ictus*. In addition to these verbal responsions the whole passage is full of military terms: in the literal statement 1046-8 *contendit, petit, saucia*; in the simile *cadunt in uulnus, comminus, hostem occupat*; in the reprise 1052-7 *telis, iaculatur, iactans, feritur, tendit, coire, iacere*. This bare list and the shape of it show what Lucretius was trying to do, but nobody seems to appreciate it. For instance *petere* and *occupare* both mean to attack very frequently in Latin but they are both rendered without any such overtone in the English translators.[18]

The primary reason for citing this passage however, is to affirm Friedländer's understanding of it. *Haec . . . hinc . . . hinc*, the origin of the name *amor*, the source of the drop of

Venus' sweetness is the *umor* which passes in the engagement of love (1051, 1056 and cf. 1065-6).[19]

Friedländer's article (summarized by Bailey 158-9) is full of such plays upon words and many of them appear to be suggested etymologies. *Religio*, for instance he connects with *religare* to bind in 4 7, and even with *caeli regione* in 1 64. I shall take his examples as read and adduce a few others, to show that there is a great wealth of such phenomena in Lucretius.

My first three examples will exemplify the onomatopoeic force with which this device can be used. In 2 257 for instance, our free will is wrested from the fates, *fatis auolsa uoluntas*, where Bailey tacitly emends to *auulsa*. The depravity of this reading would be surprising had not Bailey nailed his colours to the mast in his note on *ingenui fontes* which is what he writes for 1 230, commenting 'OQ preserve the archaic form *ingenuei*'.

Again when we let the obvious slip through our fingers in 4 504, the Latin reads *manibus manifesta suis emittere*, and the jingle of *manibus manifesta* seems to stress the obviousness of what we have lost.

Similarly in his description of the point at which parallel lines seem to meet:

donec in obscurum coni conduxit acumen.

4 431

the repeated *con* joins the four other *c* sounds in the line to sharpen the onomatopoea. For the Latin speaker this would have been rendered even more pungent by subconscious association with words like *acanthus aceo acer acerbus acetum acidus acies acinaces acontias aculeus acumen acuo acus acutus.*

Sometimes it is more of an idea play than a word play as when the topmost surface seems to be at rest in the highest stability:

summa tamen summa uideatur stare quiete

2 310

or when spiders' webs and birds' feathers and thistle down
find it often no light matter to fall:
  nimia leuitate cadunt plerumque grauatim
  3 387
Etymologies in Latin are often startlingly puerile. The
greatest scholar of Lucretius' day was M. Terentius Varro
and his work on the Latin language is full of derivations
which seem to us to be little short of imbecile. In the fifth
book of his *de Lingua Latina* he connects *umor* moisture
with *humus* earth which exudes it (24); and *Ceres* with
gerit because she *bears* the crops *quod gerit fruges* (64); and
caelum with *celatum* because the sky is *not* concealed (18);
and by a double etymology *palus* a marsh with *paululum* a
little, because the water is shallow, and *palam* openly,
because it is widely spread (26). Nor is Virgil very much
more sceptical. Bartelink has recently listed well over a hundred possible instances of etymologies implied in the *Aeneid*.

Lucretius' fascination with words is obvious where he
compares the atomic structure of the world with the letters
in a sentence. In describing how the elements occur in
different combinations to produce different results he offers
the examples of *ignes* and *lignum* (1 912) fires and wood, and
ex alienigenis quae lignis exoriuntur 1 874 is playing with
the same idea, 'from dissimilars which arise out of timbers'.
¶ *Acheron*. With these tendencies in mind we may study
two passages which show Lucretius' attitude to religion.
The first is his discussion of the torments of Hell at the end
of the third book:
  atque ea ni mirum quae cumque Acherunte profundo
  prodita sunt esse, in uita sunt omnia nobis.
  nec miser inpendens magnum timet aere saxum   980
  Tantalus, ut famast, cassa formidine torpens;
  sed magis in uita diuom metus urget inanis
  mortalis casumque timent quem cuique ferat fors.
  3 978-83

8

*And there is no doubt that all the things which are said to
occur in the depths of Hell, are here with us in this life. Nor
is there any poor Tantalus afraid of the great rock hanging
in mid air, as the story goes, paralysed by empty terror. But
rather in this life, an idle fear of the gods bears down upon
men and they are all afraid of the fate that may befall them.*

In Homer (*Odyssey* 11 582-92) Tantalus is a thirsty old
man standing up to the neck in water, but when he stoops
to drink it, it recedes, and the earth dries at his feet. From
above his head the spreading trees drop down their fruit,
pears and pomegranates, glistening apples, sweet figs and
ripe olives, but the moment he reaches up for them, the
wind tosses them up to the dark clouds.

For all his admiration of Homer, Lucretius has nothing
to do with this allegory of titillated appetites. He follows the
version common in Greek lyric and tragedy where the essential point is not the tantalizing of Tantalus but his fear.
Surely Lucretius chooses the great rock poised overhead,
because it provides such a convenient analogy for superstition, an analogy we have already noted in the etymology
proposed in 1 65, *super instans.*

So *superstitio* stands over us in the sky, and that is the
rock that hangs over Tantalus in 3 980ff. The allegory fits
the torment very closely. Tantalus' fear is *cassa*, vain;
fear of the gods is *inanis*. The rock is over his head
(*impendens*); the fear of the gods oppresses mortals (*urget*).
For this use of *urget*, compare the description of a man in his
grave oppressed and crushed by the weight of earth above him:

> urgeriue superne obrutum pondere terrae
> 3 893

Casum in 983 is a pun. While Tantalus is worried about the
fall of the rock, mortals are afraid of *casum* meaning 'chance',
'what may befall them', the notion that *Fors* can lead to a
fall being familiar from Pacuuius 368R. No doubt the
etymological play in *ferat Fors* is also operating here. *Casum*

may even be a double pun. At this stage we can but point out its resemblance to *cassum*. The Romans did not flinch from multiple etymologies.

The same vivid imagery marks the next torment:

nec Tityon uolucres ineunt Acherunte iacentem

. . .

sed Tityos nobis hic est, in amore iacentem
quem uolucres lacerant atque exest anxius angor
aut alia quauis scindunt cuppedine curae.

3 984, 992 - 4

Nor is there a Tityos lying in Acheron being penetrated by birds . . . but Tityos is here amongst us, the man lying prostrate in love whom the birds tear, that is, morbid pain gnaws at him or misery pecks at him with some other sort of desire.

The ruthless *ineunt* is the Homeric

δέρτρον ἔσω δύνοντες.

Odyssey 11 579

Tityos 984 is *iacentem* lying in Hell, whereas in 992 there is a slight shift in meaning, *iacentem* takes on as it commonly does a derogatory tone: the pain devours him (*exest*), just as the birds devour the entrails of Tityos, and *scindunt* too, suits the pecking of the birds:

num ergo aquila ita ut hice praedicant sciciderat pectus.

Accius *Didascalia* 5 (Warmington)

Surely then they are wrong in saying that an eagle had torn his breast.

This citation, which I do not find in the commentators, helps us to appreciate the force of the poetry by showing that the word has a bird reference, and also seems to provide an early Latin predecessor for Lucretius' sceptical approach to these torments.

Commentators have often been troubled by the slight illogicality in 993. 'Tityos is the lover whom the birds tear'. Logically he is not. 'He is the lover torn by desires.' This

difficulty is typical of the vigorous living exposition of
Lucretius. It would never be a stumbling block in the
spoken voice. And Lucretius climbs out of it easily with the
atque 'whom the birds tear, *that is,* morbid pain gnaws at
him or misery pecks at him'. This is another example of the
transfusion of terms already noted. It is admittedly not
formal logic, but it is equally not the sort of confusion made
by a bungling or unintelligent man. His grasp of the argument and of its details is so confident and insouciant that he
has no need to curb the surge of his imagination. If he
suddenly sees these anxieties of love as birds' beaks, then
down it goes, giving this quality of aggressiveness and
passion to his exposition.

Most of these correspondences between torment and allegory have been seen by commentators but they have not seen
how thoroughly Lucretius is doing the same with Sisyphus:

Sisyphus in uita quoque nobis ante oculos est,
qui petere a populo fasces saeuasque secures
imbibit et semper uictus tristisque recedit.

3 995-7

*Sisyphus too is in this life of ours before our eyes, the man
who takes it into his head to ask the people for the consular rods
and axes, and is always defeated and withdraws in chagrin.*

The terminology here is clearly political. *Petere* is the
stock word for standing for election; *recedere* is to demit
office, as in

qui dedit hoc hodie, cras si uolet auferet, ut si
detulerit fasces indigno, detrahet idem.
'pone, meum est', inquit: pono tristisque recedo.

Horace, *Epistles* I 16 33-5

*Who gives today, will take it back tomorrow if he wishes. In
the same way the power which confers the rods of office upon
somebody who doesn't deserve them, will take them back. 'Lay
it down, it is mine', it says. I lay it down and withdraw
in chagrin.*

This shows too that *tristis* is appropriate to the context (cf. Caes. *Bellum Ciuile* 1 4 *dolor repulsae*). In fact *repulsa*, electoral defeat, is the subject of the allegory thus far. And this is surprising. The other subjects allegorized are superstitious fear as represented by Tantalus, morbid desire by Tityos; the Danaids' leaky vessels which follow usually symbolize lust, but we have already dealt with that, so by a strange twist Lucretus bends the myth to his purpose, making it represent the insatiable longing for life – so that all three, superstition, desire, longing for life are all normal Epicurean targets. But in the torment of Sisyphus, the target we should have expected an Epicurean to aim at is not political failure, but the broader one of political ambition. It seems that Lucretius' attack has been confined to political failure out of his desire to make the sin fit the torment. Sisyphus' rock always rolls back on him. The obvious analogue is the politician who keeps standing for office and never gets in.

But Lucretius is not the man to be deflected from the proper object of attack by a little thing like that. He now switches to the normal Epicurean theme:

nam petere imperium, quod inanest nec datur umquam,
atque in eo semper durum sufferre laborem,
hoc est aduerso nixantem trudere monte   1000
saxum, quod tamen e summo iam uertice rusum
uoluitur et plani raptim petit aequora campi.

   3 998-1002

To canvass for power which is an illusion and is never given, and in that canvass endlessly to endure hard labour, that is struggling to push uphill the rock which for all your efforts rolls down again as soon as you get to the top and rushes towards the broad level plain.

'To be a candidate for power, which is an illusion and is never given', can mean only that all political power is hollow, that even those who win elections have achieved nothing.

So then when in 1001-2 we read that this is pushing a rock
uphill *quod tamen e summo iam uertice rusum uoluitur*
'which for all your efforts the moment you reach the very
summit rolls down again', we have already moved away
from political failure and are dealing with success; Roman
magistracies were normally annual tenures, in particular the
consulships which Lucretius seems to be thinking of here,
round which a tremendous political battle was being fought
at this time. To resume office you had to return to the
electorate. This is all clinched by 1002. The whole structure
of the passage has alerted us for terms which fit both the
torment and its allegorical application, and this is the
climax. The rock makes for the level plain, *plani petit
aequora campi*; and in electoral terms the candidate goes
down to the Campus Martius to stand for election again,
descendat in Campum petitor (Horace, *Odes* 3 1 11).

This suggestion, that 1002 is a pun, may receive some
support from the shape of the paragraph up to this point.
'There is no Tantalus but there are people who are afraid
of what may *befall* them' (torment then allegory with pun).
'There is no Tityos but there are people *gnawed* by anguish'
(torment then allegory with pun). Now Lucretius does *not*
go on, 'There is no Sisyphus but there are men who make
for the Campus, like Sisyphus' stone making for the
plain'. The fit here is more complicated and he arranges his
pieces more elaborately. Sisyphus is the frustrated politician, that is what is meant by pushing a rock up hill; but
even if you get it to the top, you must down again to the
Campus, that is to say even if you are elected, you must
presently demit office and prepare to fight your next
election. The simple pattern was torment allegory with pun;
here we have a double pattern, allegory with pun, *tristisque
recedit*; then elaboration of torment, ending like the others
in a pun, a more elaborate pun than the others, needing a
more elaborate build-up.

The general impression received from this study as from
our examination of the story of Phaethon in 5 396-406, is
that Lucretius did not believe these myths, but that he
could see that they corresponded to some facts of history or
of the human situation. There is no such place as Acheron.
Acheron is the torture we endure in this life. This attitude of
Lucretius has something in common with the Pythagorean
tradition, as Cumont showed, and also with Stoic allegorical
interpretations if Boyancé is right. But there is an important
distinction. Chrysippus, according to Cicero *De Natura
Deorum* 1 41, so reconciled the old poetic myths to his own
theology that he made out the ancient poets to be Stoics.
The Stoics are thus saving the myths and using them to
confirm their own ideology. Lucretius is rejecting them. As
Müller 45 argues, Lucretius is not providing an allegorical
explanation of the poetic myths, but rather arguing that
men conceive all manner of false fears and foolish desires,
and invent an underworld where these are endlessly
punished. Lucretius' point is that this underworld does not
exist and that men could be freed of their belief in it if they
could free their minds of their fears and desires.

¶ *The Earth Mother.* This is confirmed by the famous
passage on the Earth Mother, which deserves careful analysis
because none of the standard commentators seems to have
fully understood it. Lucretius has been explaining the maternity of the earth in materialistic terms. It produces everything which it does produce by the movement of the great
variety of atoms which it contains:

quare magna deum mater materque ferarum
et nostri genetrix haec dicta est corporis una.

hanc ueteres Graium docti cecinere poetae   600
sedibus in curru biiugos agitare leones,
aeris in spatio magnam pendere docentes
tellurem, neque posse in terra sistere terram.

2 598-603

This is why she is called the great mother of the gods and the mother of the animals and the one and only parent of our bodies. She it is, according to the learned poets of ancient Greece, who in her chariot seat drives her lions yoked in pair, thereby teaching that the great world hangs in airy space and that earth cannot stand on earth.

The allegory in this last sentence is very detailed. *Sedibus* is picked up by *sistere*. She is on a seat to indicate that the earth does not stand. So *in curru* is echoed by *aeris in spatio*. She is in a chariot to indicate that the earth is in airy space, and *spatio* may just carry a reference to the race course to reinforce the parallelism. The earth is called great, *magnam tellurem* to remind us of the *magna mater deum* who is being allegorized. On this passage Bailey compares Varro quoted by St. Augustine *De Ciuitate Dei* 7 24. But Varro's allegory is simpler. *Quod sedens fingatur, ipsam non moueri.* The earth is depicted as sitting to indicate that she does not move. This relates one detail of the ritual to one detail of contemporary astronomy. Lucretius is juggling with several different details of the ritual, wording them to make them fit a view held, for instance, by Empedocles which is in fact inconsistent with Epicurean cosmology.[20] Lucretius is not, as Perret believes, offering a benign and sympathetic interpretation of this myth. Nor, as Masson 390 and Regenbogen 73-4 believe, is he deeply riven between his ideological rejection of these beliefs and a temperamental affinity towards them. Lucretius does not believe in this allegory, and he makes this explicit by stating several times in this passage (612, 616, 641), that these allegories are what was meant by the *poets*. He has not soiled his own mind with these superstitions. But it is wholly in accordance with the empathetic genius of this poet, with the virulence of his polemic and with his own penchant for word play to mimic the ingenuity of this allegorizing technique. The awkwardness of the language, in particular the abruptness

of *sedibus* without an epithet, is explained by his eagerness
to adjust the rite to fit the allegory, which is very like his
habit, analysed in the previous chapter, of twisting the simile
to fit the argument. There is no need to tamper with the text.

adiunxere feras, quia quamuis effera proles
officiis debet molliri uicta parentum.

2 604-5

*The poets yoked wild beasts to her chariot because children
no matter how wild they are, ought to submit and be tamed
to the service of their parents.*

Why is the Earth Mother drawn by the wildest of her children?
The answer is that children must submit to and obey their
parents, even the wildest of children. *Mollire* is used elsewhere
of taming what is wild[21] and the point about wildness is
further illuminated by the etymological play in *feras effera.*

muralique caput summum cinxere corona,
eximiis munita locis quia sustinet urbes.

2 606-7

*And they girt the top of her head with a crown of walls because
at conspicuous points she is fortified and holds up cities.*

Every word in the rite is here allegorically interpreted. They
girt the top of Cybele's head to indicate that the earth was
fortified in conspicuous places, that is high points; with a
mural crown because she supports cities – and the Italian
reading this would be bound to think of the fortified hill
towns of Italy piled on top of their rock cliffs. *Summum
caput* is then answered not only by *eximiis locis* but also by
sustinet. Boyancé 160-1 tries to prove that this passage is
derived from Stoic theological writings, but his arguments
are too finely spun.

hanc uariae gentes antiquo more sacrorum
Idaeam uocitant matrem Phrygiasque cateruas
dant comites, quia primum ex illis finibus edunt
per terrarum orbem fruges coepisse creari.

2 610-3

Different races in their traditional rites call her the Idaean
mother and give her troops of Phrygians as an escort,
because they say that it was from Phrygian territory that
crops were first created and spread throughout the world.
Why did they give her Phryges? Because people believed
that *fruges*, crops, had their origin in that country, and
Cybele / Demeter is, of course, the goddess of grain. Lucretius
explicitly disavows responsibility for this puerile allegorizing. *Edunt* in line 612 attributes this thought to others. He
himself, in the first two lines of the sixth book, awards the
primacy in this matter to Athens and not to Phrygia. It is a
grim comment upon the present state of Lucretian scholar-
ship that none of the commentators sees this pun. They
would have if they had read the poem aloud.

    gallos attribuunt, quia, numen qui uiolarint
    Matris et ingrati genitoribus inuenti sint, ·
    significare uolunt indignos esse putandos,
    uiuam progeniem qui in oras luminis edant.

    2 614-7

They give her Galli because they wish to signify that those
who violate the divinity of the Mother and are convicted of
ingratitude towards their parents are not fit to bring live
progeny to the shores of light.
Why did they give her a retinue of emasculated young men?
Ovid offers a simple explanation in *Fasti* 4 223-44. Their
mythical model the archpriest Attis had been castrated
because he had broken the vow of celibacy which he had
made to the goddess and suffered condign punishment.
Lucretius is again more complex and elusive. The offence as
he words it, is that they have violated the divinity of their
mother and been found guilty of ingratitude towards their
parents. Boyancé 155-6 does not believe that this description can refer to the Ovidian tale. In the rich diversity of
extant versions of the Attis myth, he connects this passage
with a later story, which he attributes to the Stoics, that

Attis was the son of the goddess and was castrated as a penalty for being in love with her. Again his arguments seem to me to be wiredrawn. Lucretius is following the familiar version of the myth but wording it to assimilate the story to the allegory he is going to propound.

They violated the divinity by breaking their vow. And the verb *uiolare* is used because their punishment is that they lay violent hands upon themselves. *Uiolenti furoris* is mentioned in 621. 'Ingratitude' is a perfectly reasonable term to apply to the breach of faith as described by Ovid, but it is surely one of the difficulties of Boyancé's explana-tion that it is scarcely the *mot juste* for incestuous rape. In *matris* and *genitoribus* in 615 Lucretius is insisting that the offence is against a parent in order to assimilate the offence to the punishment. Such people have offended against their parent and been castrated to show that ungrateful children don't deserve to have children of their own.

A prudent critic would stop there. But the word *uiuam* is disturbing. Ungrateful children are not fit to have children of their own. So far so good. But *live* children? Is there any sense or justice in suggesting that ungrateful children or eunuchs for that matter, are fit only to have stillborn children? *Uiuam* of course may be a meaningless ornamental epithet, but there is a relevant fact which I cannot avoid, ridiculous though it will seem. There are *galli* whose offspring is not live. The common fowl is oviparous, and eggs are cited in 2 927-30 as a self-evident example of what is insensate. A similar point is made in a famous passage in the proem to Ennius *Annales* (10-12V). Lucretius is making the allegor-izers back two horses. *Terra mater* is given *Galli*, that is (*a*) eunuchs, (*b*) cocks, and by this they wish to signify (*significare uolunt* shows that Lucretius is having nothing to do with it) that children who are ungrateful to their parents are not fit to have (*a*) children, (*b*) live children. This etymological connection is made also by Isidore

(*Origines* 12 7 50) who suggests that cocks are called *galli* because they are the only birds which are liable to be castrated.[22]

In this passage there is more in this vein. Her retinue are called Curetes because they *play* with arms, dancing in rhythm, this depending on the closeness of the Greek word *kouroi* meaning boys. This is an ancient pun, going back in Latin to Ennius *Euhemerus*, the earliest surviving Latin literary prose. According to the doctrines of *Euhemerus*, which have had some importance in religious history, the gods were merely distinguished mortals who left behind them an imperishable memory. Venus, for instance (Ennius *fragment* 12V) was a dissolute Cretan woman who covered up her shame by inducing the women of Crete to inaugurate the oldest profession. Jupiter (*fragment* 11V) was a great ruler who died after many benefactions to mankind. Then we read that his sons the Curetes laid out his body and dressed it for burial. *Curetes filii sui curauerunt decoraueruntque eum.* Scholars have often seen the pun *Curetes curauerunt* (see Laughton), but there is also a play between *Curetes* and *filii*, *kouroi* being the link, as we saw in the Lucretius.[23] There may even be a third pun in this phrase. The word *decorauerunt* may be added to the play with the word *Curetes*. If he is capable of a double etymological pun, there is every likelihood that he is capable of tripling the play.

It is clearly easy to carry this sort of suggestion too far. In analysing these ingenuities, the scholar may well become infected by the puerility of the Latin. But there can be no doubt about the connection between *Curetes* (628-30) and *ludunt*, they are called Curetes (kouroi, boys) because they play. It is put beyond all question in line 635 where Lucretius refers to the Dictaean Curetes dancing round the infant Zeus as *pueri circum puerum pernice chorea*. There is rather more room for doubt in the suggestion of an Edinburgh

Classics student that *chorea* is a second pun, borne out to some extent by the insistence on dancing in the similar context of 631, and by the multiple puns with which the passage now ends:

propterea magnam armati matrem comitantur,
aut quia significant diuam praedicere ut armis
ac uirtute uelint patriam defendere terram
praesidioque parent decorique parentibus esse.

2 640-3

That's why they are armed as they accompany the Great Mother; or else because they mean that the goddess instructs them to be willing to defend their fatherland with their arms and their manly virtue, and to be ready to be the defence and the pride of their parents.

This passage shows that the poet is not satisfied with the strictly logical allegorizing puns, but is also hunting down puns which are not logically helpful. There they are to defend their fatherland (*patria*), and to be ready (*parent*) to defend their parents (*parentibus*).[24] This in turn suggests that other resemblances which we have pointed out in passing in this chapter *cassa casum, Curetes chorea, Curetes decorauerunt*, may not be coincidental. It may also be that the reference to *uirtus* carries with it the implication of my translation above.

There may also be in the nodding of the heads in 632

terrificas capitum quatientes nomine cristas

a reference to another tradition about the Corbyantes and Curetes (see Servius on Virgil *Aeneid* 3 111, Cybele ἀπό τοῦ κυβιστᾶν τὴν κεφαλήν i.e. *a capitis rotatione, quod proprium est eius sacerdotum*).

Lucretius, it must be repeated, does not believe in this drivel. Müller shows convincingly that he develops this line of thought purely to contrast it with his own. These are the views of the last-ditch apologists and Lucretius expressly rejects them:

quae bene et eximie quamuis disposta ferantur,
longe sunt tamen a uera ratione repulsa.   645
omnis enim per se diuom natura necessest
inmortali aeuo summa cum pace fruatur
semota ab nostris rebus seiunctaque longe;
nam priuata dolore omni, priuata periclis,
ipsa suis pollens opibus, nihil indiga nostri,   650
nec bene promeritis capitur neque tangitur ira.
terra quidem uero caret omni tempore sensu,
et quia multarum potitur primordia rerum,
multa modis multis effert in lumina solis.
hic siquis mare Neptunum Cereremque uocare   655
constituet fruges et Bacchi nomine abuti
mauolt quam laticis proprium proferre uocamen,
concedamus ut hic terrarum dictitet orbem
esse deum matrem, dum uera re tamen ipse   659
religione animum turpi contingere parcat.   680
2 644-680

*However neatly and ingeniously this is arranged and
presented, the fact remains that it is far removed from true
reasoning. For all divinity by its very nature must of neces-
sity enjoy its immortal life in supreme calm far removed
from our concerns and dissevered from them. Immune from
pain and immune from danger, sufficient by its own
resources and requiring nothing from us, it is not put under
an obligation to us by any services we may render it, nor is it
touched by anger. But the earth in fact is always insensate
and it is because it possesses the atoms of many things that
it brings many things out into the light of the sun in many
different ways. This being so, if anybody decides to call the
sea Neptune or bread Ceres or prefers to use the name
Bacchus rather than employ the literal term for the liquid,
let us allow him to call the earth the mother of the gods,
provided however, that he himself does not taint his mind
with rotten superstition.*

This whole excursus is carefully locked into context (see Müller 44 as against Giussani and Perret). Its purpose is to contrast the mythological account of Mother Earth and its allegories with the Epicurean truth. This truth, that the earth has within it the elements from which everything is made, is stated from line 589 onward, and resumed in similar terms after the excursus in 652-59. Typically enough, in both of these passages where the logician would be using literal language, the poet produces a term which hints at metaphor from childbirth, *extollere* in 595 and *effert* in 654. Lucretius explains precisely what he means by the maternity of the earth so he feels free here and in many other passages to indulge his poetic enjoyment of the metaphor. He can even make the assertion, astonishing in Epicurean terms, that we are all sprung from heavenly seed (2 991-7), the sky is our father, the earth receives his moisture and conceives and bears and feeds. All this we have already seen as a metaphor in the second chapter, on 1 250-61, and it recurs in the paragraph in 5 796-836 with a cosmogonical interpretation: in her youth when her husband was in full vigour and there were more heat and moisture in her furrows the earth was more productive, but nowadays her only spontaneous generation is of creatures like worms. In those days wombs were rooted in the earth, and the young emerged when their time came. Earth turned towards them nipples full of a juice like milk. She fed them, clothed them, and bedded them with the vegetation she supplied. But now she is past bearing. In this passage, which I have discussed at length in the *Classical Review*, the ambivalent details, the puns and the similes all make it quite obvious that Lucretius was fascinated by this meta-phor. But metaphor it always is for him. The earth is not a woman or a goddess, but a lump of insensate matter. It is not the business of the gods to labour like this, and in the passage just quoted Lucretius systematically refutes the

allegorizing that has preceded. The Earth Mother does not
need attendants because the god's lives are far removed
from our affairs (2 648). She could not suffer an everlasting
wound because the gods are exempt from all pain (2 649).
She does not need an armed escort because gods are immune
from all danger (2 649). She does not need financial contributions from us because the gods' might is based upon their
own resources (2 650 *ipsa suis pollens opibus*), in fact in
Varro 5 64 we are told that the Earth is called Ops. The gods
are not put under an obligation by any services we can render nor are they touched by any anger. Nothing can reach
them to ruffle their serenity or impair their perfection.
Hence his scorn for priests and rites and petitionary prayers
and his loathing for the fear and misery occasioned by false
doctrine about the gods. Not that this can harm their bliss.
They are immune even from our heresies. But if we think
like this we can deprive ourselves of the blessings which
religion has to offer.

Byron said perhaps mockingly, that Don Juan's mother
was afraid that Lucretius' irreligion was too strong for early
stomachs. To Dryden he was so much an atheist, that he
forgot sometimes to be a poet. According to E. B. Browning
he denied divinely the divine. Despite such pronouncements
there is no irreligion or atheism in Lucretius. The deeply
religious experience of Epicureanism lay in communion. By
contemplating the perfection of the gods in prayer and
trance and dream we could enjoy and share that perfection
and carry back to our own lives some portion of it. Lucretius
states his doctrine explicitly in 6 68-79, and it is necessary
to the understanding of much of his poetry, including a
passage which we have so far passed over in this study of the
allegory of the Earth Mother:

tympana tenta tonant palmis et cymbala circum
concaua, raucisonoque minantur cornua cantu,
et Phrygio stimulat numero caua tibia mentis,   620

telaque praeportant, uiolenti signa furoris,
ingratos animos atque impia pectora uolgi
conterrere metu quae possint numine diuae.
ergo cum primum magnas inuecta per urbis
munificat tacita mortalis muta salute,   625
aere atque argento sternunt iter omne uiarum
largifica stipe ditantes ninguntque rosarum
floribus umbrantes matrem comitumque cateruas.

2 618-28
*The taut drums thunder under their palms, the round con-
caves of the cymbals clash, the hoarse menacing note of the
horns resounds and the hollow pipe goads the mind with its
Phrygian rhythms, as they hold up before them the weapons
which are tokens of madness and violence, to terrify the
ungrateful and impious hearts of the people with fear of the
goddess's divinity. And so as soon as she is carried in
procession through great cities and quietly bestows her
silent salvation, they strew her whole route with silver and
bronze enriching it with their generous contributions and
snowing down rose petals to shade the goddess and her troops
of acolytes.*

These eleven lines are not simply a description of a
religious procession. Cybele's orchestra is heard also in the
fragments of Varro and in Catullus 64. But whereas the
performance in Catullus occurs in a learned and richly
gilded remaniement of a myth which it is not easy to care
much about, in Lucretius the music is part of feelings and
thoughts which clearly moved the poet and can move us.
The music is there for the stillness which follows it in 625.
And just as *tacita* and *muta* hark back to the blaring clangour
of the orchestra, and forward to the clatter of money on the
street, contrasting the public hocus-pocus with the private
blessing of communion, so does *munificat* in the same great
line contrast the true gift of the goddess with the *parua stips*
of a street collection (so called in Ovid *Fasti* 4 350), but

9

described by Lucretius in an epic fortissimo. *Munificat tacita mortalis muta salute* is not to me at any rate ironic, as Giussani suggests in his commentary. Lucretius is acknowledging religious emotion while ridiculing superstitious ceremonial.

He is also ridiculing superstitious fear. In 621-3 the weapons exhibited by these eunuchs as tokens of their madness and violence are said to be able to terrify the *ungrateful* minds and impious hearts of the people by the *divinity* of the goddess. Now, we are keyed in to allegories. So we remember line 614-5 which suggest that the castrated Galli represent those who have violated the *divinity* of the Mother goddess and have been *ungrateful* to their parents. For those whose sin is the same as the sin of the Galli, there can be no mistaking the menace of these swishing blades.

9. The Poetry

¶ *Sound.* This book has attempted to show how the poetry of Lucretius works by studying his imagery. But there is a lot more to the poetry than that. This last chapter will broaden the scope of our study by indicating two other factors which contribute to the poetry, its sound and its passion. Even here we are not going very far from the imagery. What we have been looking at is the product of Lucretius' faculty for association, and as we move on to consider the passion which fills the whole poem and the collusion between the sound and sense of the verses, we are still concerned with Lucretius' associative faculty, and the excitement and delight he finds in it and gives with it.

The alliteration and onomatopoea in the poem have already been analysed in Deutsch's second chapter, and by Bailey in his preface 119-20 and 146-52, and everybody is familiar with the direct imitation of sound by sound in Lucretius, where, for example, multiple alliteration imitates the sound of wind or saw or a howling baby, *uentorum ualidis feruescunt uiribus undae* 3 494, *serrae stridentis acerbum horrorem* 2 410-1, *uagituque locum lugubri complet* 5 226. Equally familiar is the less direct, synaesthetic imita-tion of some other sensory stimuli by the sound of Lucretius' verse, the look of a rickety structure, the bitter taste of wormwood, the feel of the boring of holes, the smell of dead

bodies, *praua cubantia prona supina atque absona tecta* 4 517,
at contra taetra absinthi natura 2 400, *et terebrare etiam
pertundere perque forare* 5 1268, *taetra cadauera torrent* 2 415.
But there is still something to be said about onomatopoea
which is even less directly imitative, about alliterations
which accompany something other than sensory stimuli,
about metrical and syntactical shapes in the Latin which
correspond with intellectual concepts or emotional states
or with the structure of Lucretius' arguments. Some such
correspondences are clearly shown in a typical technical
argument where Lucretius is explaining how the parts of the
world as we know it separated out from a compact mass of
atoms:

> . . . sic igitur terrae concreto corpore pondus
> constitit atque omnis mundi quasi limus in imum
> confluxit grauis et subsedit funditus ut faex;
> inde mare, inde aër, inde aether ignifer ipse
> corporibus liquidis sunt omnia pura relicta
> et leuiora aliis alia, et liquidissimus aether   500
> atque leuissimus aerias super influit auras
> nec liquidum corpus turbantibus aeris auris
> commiscet; sinit haec uiolentis omnia uerti
> turbinibus, sinit incertis turbare procellis,
> ipse suos ignis certo fert impete labens.   505
> nam modice fluere atque uno posse aethera nisu
> significat Pontos, mare certo quod fluit aestu
> unum labendi conseruans usque tenorem.

   5 495-508

*So then the weight of the earth formed a hard mass and came
to rest and being heavy flowed together to the bottom of the
whole world like slime, and settled down in the depths like the
dregs of wine. From this the liquid bodies of sea, then of air,
then of the fire-bearing aether itself were all left pure, each
lighter than the other, and the aether most liquid of all and*

the lightest flowed over the breezes of the air and did not mix its liquid substance with the turbulent breezes of the air. It allows all this to be whirled around by violent winds, it allows it all to be stirred by irregular storms, while on its own regular motion it glides along bearing its own fires with it. That the aether can flow along in a constant moderate motion, is proved by the Pontus, the sea that flows with one fixed tide always maintaining the constant tenour of its gliding.

In this passage alliterative, metrical and syntactical onomatopoea are all richly combined. The plosives in the first line for the hardening of the earth are followed by nine liquids and four long *i*'s in eleven syllables for the slime, *omnis mundi quasi limus in imum*. And so on throughout the passage.

Similarly, two unusual metrical phenomena are set to vigorous onomatopoeic work. The monosyllabic ending at the end of 497 corresponds with the settling of sludge, and the only line in the paragraph to start with nine long syllables corresponds with the maintenance of the endless, even tenour of the gliding of the Hellespont. But the normal anatomy of the metre is just as important. The first three lines describing the formation of the earth are broken by powerful and progressive enjambements, as *constitit* and *confluxit grauis* start successive lines. The lines describing the separating out of the liquid entities are all more end-stopt until the mention of mixture in *commiscet* 503. Then the turbulence of the winds is described in two lines where the repeated *sinit* feints at a disturbance of the normal line division, whereas in 505 the evenness and independence of the aether is conveyed in a very unusual rhythm in a line starting with four two-syllable words.

Apart from these metrical facts, there are syntactical shapes which are also operating as the poetry is read or heard. As the progressive lightness and ascension of sea, air

and aether is described, in 498 there is a progressive
lengthening of phrase, an ascending tricolon with anaphora
of *inde mare, inde aer, inde aether ignifer ipse*; a similar
ascending tricolon with anaphora of *et* is hinted at by
499-500 although the logic is slightly different. Here the
ascension is marked syntactically also by the ascension of
the adjectives from positive to comparative to superlative,
from *liquidis* to *leuiora* to *liquidissimus atque leuissimus*.
The gliding of the Pontus in 508 is marked by the hyper-
baton of *unum* . . . *tenorem* producing a line similar in shape
to one type of the golden line with which Catullus and many
other Roman poets so often point their climaxes:

    annuus exactis completur mensibus orbis
       Virgil *Aeneid* 5 46
or
    ingens accedit stomacho fultura ruenti
       Horace *Satires* 2 3 154
where massive scaffolding arrives to shore up a toppling
stomach.

It may be felt that these metrical and syntactical phenomena are accidental or inert, and that these alleged correspondences are of no importance to the poetry. There is
after all no direct imitation here; the relationship posited
between sound and sense is so subtle and so devious that
the sceptic may feel that critics will be able to detect such
relationships in shopping lists. Admittedly this indirect
onomatopoea is very difficult to study systematically or
safely, but it is in my experience so important to the effect
of the poetry that I shall try to establish the validity of it
by some shorter examples.

In 1 514 only solid matter can have void concealed within
its body and the word order imitates this, *corpore inane suo
celare*. In 1 835-7 where bones are composed of tiny pieces
of bone and flesh of tiny pieces of flesh, the line about bone
has the same sound and appearance as the line about flesh

ossa uidelicet e pauxillis atque minutis
ossibus hic et de pauxillis atque minutis
uisceribus uiscus gigni
Lucretius 3 159, describing the close relationships between
spirit and mind, and mind and body, is the only line in the
entire corpus of epic poetry from Cicero to Silius where
the preposition *cum* is elided, and there it is elided
twice:
esse animam cum animo coniunctam quae cum animi ui
percussast, exim corpus propellit et icit.
In 4 1259 where thick is mixed with clear and clear with
thick, the first syllable of *liquidis* is short and the first
syllable of *liquida* is long:
crassaque conueniant liquidis et liquida crassis.
In 1 1012-3 the limitlessness of space or of matter is physically represented in the great distance between *alterutrum*
and *immoderatum*:
aut etiam alterutrum, nisi terminet alterum, eorum
simplice natura pateat tamen immoderatum
and in 1 1014-6 by a poetic Morton's fork a similar hyper-
baton of *exiguum* and *tempus* makes more appalling the
brief moment that the massive edifice of our world could
survive if matter were finite:
nec mare nec tellus neque caeli lucida templa
nec mortale genus nec diuum corpora sancta
exiguum possent horai sistere tempus.
In 1 814-6 many things have similar atoms in different
combinations and the Latin has three similar items in
different relationships:
ni mirum quia multa modis communia multis
multarum rerum in rebus primordia mixta
sunt, ideo uariis uariae res rebus aluntur.
This effective juxtaposition of the same word in different
cases, polyptoton is the technical term for it, may be classed
as a form of syntactical onomatopoea and it is very common

and effective in Lucretius, as in Ovid and other Latin poets.
At 2 174-6 we are told that those who imagine that the
gods made *every*thing are in *every* way *far* from the truth:

quorum omnia causa
constituisse deos cum fingunt, omnibus rebus
magno opere a uera lapsi ratione uidentur.

This polyptoton occurs with negatives at 2 235-6, where
Lucretius is arguing that empty void can *never* support *anything anywhere, nulli de nulla parte neque ullo tempore*, and at
2 239 where bodies of unequal weight move at equal speed

aeque ponderibus non aequis concita ferri.

It is occasionally combined with puns, as in 2 310 where, as
we have seen, the uppermost surface of things is at rest in
highest stillness

summa tamen summa uideatur stare quiete

and in 3 364 where bright lights dazzle our bright eyes

lumina luminibus quia nobis praepediuntur.[25]

In 2 1054, *innumero numero summaque profunda*, the pun
on *summa* is pointed not by polyptoton but by the symmetry of the expression. The atoms are in innumerable
number and in the unfathomed sum of things, where the
shape of the syntax forces you to remember that *summa*
can mean not only the universe but also the opposite of
profunda, forces you to entertain the weird paradox of 'the
bottommost surface'.

Any attempt to talk about this interaction of sound and
sense is doomed to be slow and clumsy. But it is the source
of much of the power and pungency of this poetry, and
since writers on Lucretius have not done justice to it, such
analysis seems to be necessary. Too often the critics have
contented themselves with pouncing on Lucretius for his
'banalities' and 'spirited crudities' wherever he produces a
rhythm Virgil would not have written. Even lovers of
Lucretius are too ready to apologise. Ernout for example,
in the introduction to his commentary gives five passages

which seem to him to exhibit Lucretian imperfections. The
first is 1 236 whose sound, far from being imperfect, is richly
effective in its context. Lucretius is arguing for the indestructibility of the atoms:

praeterea quae cumque uetustate amouet aetas,
si penitus peremit consumens materiem omnem,
unde animale genus generatim in lumina uitae
redducit Venus, aut redductum daedala tellus
unde alit atque auget generatim pabula praebens?
unde mare ingenuei fontes externaque longe   230
flumina suppeditant? unde aether sidera pascit?
omnia enim debet, mortali corpore quae sunt,
infinita aetas consumpse ante acta diesque.
quod si in eo spatio atque ante acta aetate fuere
e quibus haec rerum consistit summa refecta,   235
inmortali sunt natura praedita certe.
haud igitur possunt ad nilum quaeque reuerti.
    1 225-37

*Further, if everything that old age and time remove is utterly
destroyed and its substance consumed whence does Venus
lead back the families of animals generation by generation to
the light of life? And when they have been brought back whence
does the richly-varied earth nourish and increase them
generation by generation with its sustenance? Whence is the
sea supplied by the springs within it and rivers without, rising
at their distant sources? Whence does the aether feed the stars?
For the infinity of past time and eternity must have consumed every mortal body.*

*So if there have existed in all the expanse of time past
the bodies from which the universe is composed and recom-
posed, they are surely endowed with immortality. Therefore
none of the atoms can return to nothing.*

The argument in this paragraph is as follows:

  1. If matter is destructible,
  2. How are earth, sea and sky supplied?

3. Infinite time past would have consumed them all.
4. So if the atoms have survived all that time,
5. They are immortal.

The second element is this argument is expressed in three highly organized rhetorical questions. Earth is covered in three lines, in two questions linked by verbal repetitions, *unde, generatim, redducere.* Sea is given a line and a half with *unde* again. Sky is a half line, and it continues the anaphora with *unde.* It is unusual in Latin to find a run of anaphoric clauses decreasing in length. The ascending tricolon with anaphora is the normal pattern. But this is not a weakness. The argument is gathering pace throughout these questions until in line 232 *omnia* collects them all together and the sentences end in 233 with the slow and weighty statement of the third element set out above. Here the sense, the syntax and the metre are conspiring to make argumentation poetic. After the variety and the lightening rhythms of the syntax in the passage which deals with life and nourishment, the infinity of time past is expressed with imitative abundance *infinita aetas ante acta diesque* broken only by the concept of consumption in *consumpse*; after the dactyls in the preceding lines the climax comes in this line which begins with nine long syllables. This rhythm has an echo in the last two elements of the argument, *inmortali sunt natura praedita certe,* and this is the line for which Ernout apologizes. To suggest that the nine long syllables in this line are due to negligence, insouciance or the inability to do anything else is the deaf application of handbook rules to the Lucretian hexameter.

The same is true for all of his examples. Admittedly *infinitus* and *immortalis* will most frequently appear as four long syllables, and it was convenient for Lucretius to round off lines with *materiai* and *principiorum*. But a sympathetic reading, which is more probative than all this argumentation, will show that again and again the poet is

moulding his material to match the movement of his argument, and so charging that argument with poetry. In the
face of lines like the three which I am about to quote, it is
wrong to talk, as Ernout does, of 'négligence . . . ou plutôt
insouciance, et peut-être aussi impuissance de faire autre-
ment'. Apology is out of place. After listening to the voice of
the critics, listen to the voice of Lucretius

uersibus ostendens corpuscula materiai
ex infinito summam rerum usque tenere
undique protelo plagarum continuato.

2 529-31

*showing in his verse that from infinite time the material
atoms maintain for ever the sum of things, with an endless
series of blows like an endless line of oxen coming in from all
sides.*

We have often found Lucretius mimicking his opponents;
but if the contention of this chapter is correct his mimicry
extends to the whole universe, including the dynamics of
his own arguments.

¶*Passion.* Lucretius is a poet of the world. Part of his mission
is to give an explanation of everything we see and feel. The
explanation is in terms of the imperceptible movements of
imperceptible particles and his main method of argument is
to explain the invisible by analogy with the visible. So the
world is his subject matter and the stockpile of his argument.
He explains life and growth and disease and death as movements of atoms, and he explains the movements of atoms
in terms of wind, waters, war and the scooping of poppy
seed. To make good the Atomic Theory, every physical
fact in the world has to be explained in atomic terms; to be
comprehensible, the atomic processes have to be compared
with the world as we perceive it.

And what a world it is! where there are snakes which eat
themselves if touched by human spittle, where goats thrive
on hemlock, where stags are thought to draw snakes from

their holes by breathing in, where lions cannot abide the sight of a cock and all this has to be explicable in terms of Atomic Theory (4 638-9, 5 899, 6 765-6, 4 710-7). Apart from such curious lore we have technical arguments which explain why a concave mirror does not reverse the image, why the magnet repels iron filings in a bronze bowl, why the sun and moon are no larger than they appear to be (4 311-7, 6 1042-64, 5 564-89), and all through the poem vivid descriptions of objects and processes of daily life and work, scooping pans on water wheels, the use of an odour- less oil as a base in perfumery, the keen-scentedness of geese (5 516, 2 850, 4 682-3).

None of this is otiose ornament. Nothing could be further from the truth than Robert Graves' conception of Lucretius. 'In didactic verse, where a sudden doubt arises and the teacher admits himself a blind groper after truth (so Lucretius time and time again) and breaks his main argument in digressions after loveliness and terror, only then does Poetry appear.' Lucretius never doubts or gropes after truth or indulges in digressions after loveliness and terror. This vast deployment of intelligence and observation is all for a purpose and that purpose is never lost to view. Every argument and every appeal to the senses and every persuasion in the poetry is subordinated to Lucretius' passionate over-riding ambition to excise the power of the gods from our picture of the world, to show that materialistic hypotheses are enough, that there is no area of the universe where we need to posit supernatural intervention, that ambition and luxury and priest-ridden fear of the gods and of punishment in an after-life, all these afflictions which destroy the peace and happiness of human beings are philosophically unnecessary and absurd. Much of the detail of Epicureanism is obsolete, but some still touches our lives closely enough to make it easy to respond emotionally to it.

This is not to say that every line in Lucretius is an

emotional experience. Much of his poetry is prosy. But this
doesn't matter. In this long work containing some of the
sublimest of all poetry, the lower reaches of the argument
are effective landscaping for these great peaks. We must
be careful before castigating the banality of even the most
functional lines.

The most notorious of these is perhaps

nunc et Anaxagorae scrutemur homoeomerian

1 830

and even here the poet is in league with the logician.
Lucretius normally avoids the use of Greek philosophical
terminology, but here he capitulates and transliterates the
Greek. Even here, however, there is a metrical effect to be
noticed. In using two Greek proper names in a line with an
unusual rhythm at the end, Lucretius is not just versifying
under duress. A glance at Catullus 64 shows that such pro -
cedures are already being sought after as deliberate effects
in Latin poetry. Nor should one throw away the force of
scrutemur. This word implies a search into the hidden details
of something, a search beneath the surface. Since the theory
of homoeomeria is that every substance is composed of a
congeries of particles of itself, *scrutemur* is a live poetic word.
Bailey is alert to that in translating 'Let us now search into
the homoeomeria of Anaxagoras'.

Even in the flattest lines there is a virtue. When at the
beginning of the fourth book after his soaring assertion of
his originality as a poet, of his eagerness to untie the tight
knots of superstition, of the darkness of his subject, the
light of his poetry and the charm of the Muses, he drags it
all down to the ground by saying that even this doesn't
seem to be wholly pointless:

id quoque enim non ab nulla ratione uidetur.

4 10

The brutal prosiness of this line is not a bathos or a banality
which we need to deplore. It is a gritty reminder that this is

a serious undertaking. Lucretius has a passion for the truth and for the liberation of men's minds. The very absence of poetic elevation in these and similar passages is part and proof of this passionate seriousness which is a rare quality among Latin poets. We should not regret or disparage such tough-minded elements in this poem but value their contribution to the effect of the whole, in intensifying its strenuous earnestness. The notion of what is improper in poetry is an unnecessary anachronism which still hinders our appreciation of Lucretius. Contemporary poets have thrown it away and use everything that comes to hand. We should exult in Lucretius' freedom and truth and not tut-tut over his improprieties.

Here we are at the heart of the *De Rerum Natura*, its emotional impact, and there is not much the critic can do to help. He can clear away the rubbish of adverse value judgments deposited by previous critics, but he cannot nowadays interest his readers in his own emotional reactions to the text. When Schubert was asked by a lady admirer the meaning of one of his minuets he went over to the piano and played it again. According to Penrose, when Picasso was pestered in the same way by three earnest Germans, he drew his revolver and fired several shots in the air. Ultimately the literary critic can't do very much more. But the passions of Lucretius were directed towards a philosophy, and the critic may be able to help readers to respond more sympathetically if he understands that philosophy and can elucidate its relevance to the poetry. It would be silly to try to convey what Lucretius felt about the night sky, but it may be useful to draw attention to the importance of astronomical ideas to the philosophies which Epicureanism was attacking. In the last passage we shall look at, the effects of onomatopoea alliterative, metrical and syntactical, are obvious to the ear, but a proper response to the poetry is not possible unless we remember the intellectual basis of the passion which gives it greatness:

ergo perfugium sibi habebant omnia diuis
tradere et illorum nutu facere omnia flecti.
in caeloque deum sedes et templa locarunt,
per caelum uolui quia nox et luna uidetur,
luna dies et nox et noctis signa seuera   1190
noctiuagaeque faces caeli flammaeque uolantes,
nubila sol imbres nix uenti fulmina grando
et rapidi fremitus et murmura magna minarum.
   5 1186-93
And so they took refuge in consigning everything to the
gods and making everything be directed by their nod, and
they put the seats and regions of the gods in the sky because
the night and the moon seemed to go round the sky, the moon,
the day and the night and austere signs of night, the night-
moving torches of the sky and the flying flames, clouds sun
showers snow winds lightnings hail and the rapid roar and
mighty murmuring of the threat of thunder.
This is not a Lucretian lollipop to sweeten the exhausted
reader. The basic doctrinal point against which Lucretius
has set his face is the notion of an astral deity, and Lucretius
knows (and indeed is about to argue) that the most powerful argument in defence of this notion is the great awe we
feel under a starlit sky, and the frisson of terror we feel in a
thunderstorm.
   This explains the omission of the sun in 1189. It is the
night and the moon rolling round the sky which strike awe
into us. The phenomena of the day will be mentioned in
due course to complete the impression of the variety and
vastness of the heavens, but initially it is the fear of the
night that daunts us. The late arrival of the sun which worried
Paul Maas is no difficulty at all, and Dean Inge's conjecture
of *sol* for *nox* is an injury to the poetry. So too is the suggestion of Diels
      per caelum quia sol et luna uidetur
      inde dies et nox

This produces an ordered alternation of sun and moon and day and night but there is no call for a chronological order to these phenomena. Similarly Lambinus' dew *ros* instead of sun *sol* in 1192 makes a more homogeneous list. But fear is the key to this passage and there is nothing intimidating about dew. Bailey concludes on page 1757 that 'the passage is anyhow confused and would probably have been altered in revision'.

This is dismal. This whole passage has its own order in terms of Lucretius' normal style and master passion. The affective repetitions of *luna* and of *nox nox noctis* and *noctiuagae* are thoroughly in his manner as analysed by Deutsch (31, 53, 57). The obsession with the night sky is thoroughly consonant with his campaign against the astral gods. If the sudden intrusion of *dies* amongst these nocturnal phenomena requires any explanation, it is offered by Gius-sani, who sees that Lucretius realizes in mid flow that not only night has its majesty. All this is characteristic of Lucretius' abundance and impetus and it is monstrous to try to shackle these to pedantic logic.

This poetry combines intelligence, sense and passion, each to a degree which we do not encounter elsewhere in Latin. And we have a long way to go before we understand it.

References

Page 3[1]. For *insitus* used with *florere* see 1 900-1 and 5 1164-5; with *gignere* 5 181-2. The fig tree bursts the tomb in Juvenal 10 145, see Mayor *ad loc.*

Page 3[2]. The image of the disturbed dregs stretches from 3 36-40 from *claranda* to *puramque*. Regenbogen 35 would confine it to line 38 mainly on the ground that similar imaginative conceptions, 'Phantasievorstellungen', never play a part anywhere else in the poetry of Lucretius. But this conception occurs at 1 987-96, 5 449-94, 1141-2, and is very frequent in other Latin poetry, for example Plautus *Aulularia* 79-80 *defaecato . . . perspexi, Trinummus* 297-300 *faeceos mores . . . consident*, Horace *Satires* 1 1 59-60, 2 4 55-7. On *liquidam* cf. the metaphorical use of *deliquare* in early Latin and Varro *de Lingua Latina* 7 106 *turbida quae sunt deliquantur, ut liquida fiant.* For *suffundere* in its precise force cf. Lucretius 6 479.

Page 7[3]. *Encyclopedia Britannica* 28 179 s.v. volcano. For the eruptions of Etna see A. S. Pease on Cicero *De Natura Deorum* 2 96. I have accepted Solmsen's reading of 1 724.

Page 33[4]. The comma which the editors print after 118 is irrational. Lucretius is suggesting that Ennius is the first Latin poet, not the first poet.

Page 45[5]. For *lumen decurrere* of the sun, cf. *decurrere luces* Tibullus 3 7 160.

Page 52[6]. With *rapax . . . raptauit* compare *rapidum . . . rapidus raptori* Plautus *Menaechmi* 64-5, and *rapidus uorat* Virgil *Aeneid* 1 117. For such *figurae etymologicae* in Plautus see Leo, in Lucretius see McCartney.

Page 56[7]. For other double images see the collapsing house and the burning house 4 866-76, the dark and the storm 5 11-12, the cracked pot and the dirty pot 6 18-25.

Page 59[8]. On the Astral religion of Aristotle and Lucretius' polemic against it see Bignone 2 407-36, Farrington in 'Science and Politics' and 'The Faith of Epicurus', and Festugière.

Page 60[9]. For *compressit* picking up *oppressa*, cf. 6 53 *depressosque premunt.*

10

Page 62[10]. The literal force of *tendere* seems not to have been lost upon Persius in his adaptation of this image (1 65-6). Compare too pariterque oculos telumque tetendit, Virgil *Aeneid* 5 508.

Page 63[11]. Nor is it easy to see what he means by his other examples. The teeth of death in 1 852 suggest that death is a monster. What species of monster is not disclosed, but there is nothing 'pure' about the teeth. In the previous line *oppressus* is the mot juste for the grinding of teeth on a hard object (cf. 3 694). The source of the imagery in his other example, the gate of death, has already been fully explained in 1 1102-13.

Page 72[12]. In my translation of 5 103 I omit the *-que* to clarify the anatomy. The mind is in the breast (3 140).

Page 80[13]. Munro too has the wrong reading, but his translation offers the right sense, 'amid such thick darkness'.

Page 82[14]. Compare *exorsa haec tela* Plaut. *Bacch.* 350. On this weaving metaphor see Bailey 1756.

Page 92[15]. For *diuerberat* suggesting swimming, cf. Ovid *Heroides* 18 80, 19 48, *Metamorphoses* 4 708, *dimouere*. The atoms swim through the air *tranantibus auras* in Lucretius 4 177. Roos also rejects Sandbach's emendation.

Page 92[16]. For other examples of such fluidity, cf. 1 348-55; and also 5 1375, 6 392, 6 796 with Sullwold's comments pp. 24 and 115. 4 1036 may be similarly linked with 1050-1.

Page 93[17]. There is nothing original about this. Housman, for instance, does it twice in two successive pages of his elucidations of Persius' sixth Satire.

Page 95[18]. For the military force of *occupare* cf. the dictionaries and Plautus *Mercator* 124 *seditionem facit lien : occupat praecordia*.

Page 96[19]. For *amor umor* cf. Plautus *Miles Gloriosus* 640, and *fragmenta dubia* 1-2.

Page 104[20]. Lucretius 1 1077-8 and Bailey *ad loc.*, and 5 554-5, Empedocles DK 31a 30. See Bignone 2 497-9 and Furley for the importance of the Peripatetic view.

Page 105[21]. Virgil *Georgics* 2 36, Ovid *Tristia* 4 1 6, and *Fasti* 4 217, where Ovid is expounding the same allegory.

Page 108[22]. The same pun occurs in Martial 3 24 and 13 63. *Galli* is used punningly of capons and Gauls by Cicero *in Pisoném* 67, in the passages there cited by Nisbet, and in Plautus *Aulularia* 472 according to Schutter. In Martial 11 74 it is used of eunuch priests and Gauls.

Page 108²³. Indeed *filii sui* would be the natural Latin translation of the Greek Διὸς Κοῦροι. For the equivalence see Weinstock's discussion of the word *qurois* in an archaic inscription
from Latium.

Page 109²⁴. Cf. *patriam parentes* Plautus *Persa* 620. Similar
plays are very common in Latin comedy, *parta patria* Naevius
84R, *patria partisset* Afranius 50R, *patres patrium* Naevius
93R, *patria patris* Turpilius 91R.

Page 120²⁵. *lumen* is subjected to punning also at 3 414 and
5 777-8.

Bibliography

If a work has been cited once only in the text, this index provides the page reference in that work. If a work has been cited more than once, the page references have been given in the text.

W.S. Anderson 'Discontinuity in Lucretian symbolism' *Transactions of the American Philological Association* 91 (1960) 1-29.

J. Armstrong *Taste* (1770) 143-4, 145-6.

R.G. Austin *'Virgil Aeneid* 2' (1964).

C. Bailey *Titi Lucreti Cari De Rerum Natura* (1949).
'Lucretius' *British Academy Lecture* (1949) 12.

H. Bardon, 'L'obstacle: métaphore et comparaison en latin' *Latomus* 23 (1964) 16.

G.J.M. Bartelink *Etymologisering bij Vergilius* (1965).

E. Bignone *L'Aristotele perduto* (1936).

P. Boyancé 'Une exégèse stoïcienne chez Lucrèce' *Revue des études latines* 19 (1941) 147-66.

P. Boyancé *Lucrèce et l'Epicurisme* (1963).

A.D. Fitton Brown *Classical Review* 2 (1952) 229.

E.B. Browning *A Vision of Poets* 337-8.

Byron *Don Juan* canto 1 stanza 43.

F. Cumont 'Lucrèce et le symbolisme pythagoricien des enfers' *Revue de Philologie* 44 (1920) 229-40.

Dante *Purgatorio* 22 67-9.

H.S. Davies 'Notes on Lucretius' *The Criterion* 11 (1931) 25-42.

R.E. Deutsch *The Pattern of Sound in Lucretius* Diss. Bryn Mawr (1939).

H. Diels *Titi Lucreti Cari De Rerum Natura* (1923-4).

Dryden *Apology for Heroic Poetry and Poetic Licence* (1677).
Poems from Sylvae (1685) Preface.

D.R. Dudley (Editor) *Lucretius* (1965) including contributions by Spencer, Townend and Wormell cited under their names.

P. Einarsson *The Surtsey Eruption* (1965).

Emerson *Essays, The Poet* (1841-5).

Encyclopedia Britannica (1910-11)[11] vol. 28 p. 179.

A. Ernout *Lucrèce De la Nature;* texte établi et traduit (1948)[2].
Lucrèce De Rerum Natura commentaire (1962)[2] (with A. Robin).

B. Farrington *Primum Graius homo* (1927) 32-4.
Science and Politics in the Ancient World (1939) 103-5, 144-5.
The Faith of Epicurus (1967) 72-5, 79, 83-7.

A.-J. Festugière *Epicure et ses dieux* (1946) translated by C.W. Chilton (1955) chapter 5.

E.M. Forster *Howards End* (1910) title page.

S. Fraisse *L'influence de Lucrèce en France au seizième siècle* (1962) 84.

P. Friedländer 'The pattern of sound and atomistic theory in Lucretius' *American Journal of Philology* 62 (1941) 18.

D.J. Furley 'Lucretius and the Stoics' *Bulletin of the Institute of Classical Studies* 13 (1966) 13-33.

F. Giancotti *Il preludio di Lucrezio* (1959) 85-90.

C. Giussani *Titi Lucreti Cari De Rerum Natura* (1896-8), in part revised by Stampini (1921-9).

R. Graves *On English Poetry* (1922).

O. Gross *De metonymis sermonis Latini a deorum nominibus petitis* Diss. Halle (1911).

A.E. Housman 'Notes on Persius' *Classical Quarterly* 7 (1913) 31-2.

W.R. Inge 'Two notes on Lucretius' *Classical Review* 54 (1940) 188.

W. James *Varieties of Religious Experience* (1902) lectures 9 and 10.

H. Klepl *Lukrez und Virgil in ihren Lehrgedichten* Diss. Leipzig (1940), reprinted Darmstadt (1967) 13-20.

F. Klingner *Römische Geisteswelt* (1956) 185-8.

W.F. Jackson Knight *Virgil Aeneid* (1956).

D. Lambinus *Titi Lucreti Cari De Rerum Natura* (1570)[4].

R.E. Latham *Lucretius on the Nature of the Universe* (1951).

E. Laughton 'The prose of Ennius' *Eranos* 49 (1951) 39 n2.

F. Leo *Analecta Plautina* (1898), reprinted in *Ausgewahlte Kleine Schriften* vol. 1 (1960).

W.E. Leonard *Lucretius: Of the Nature of Things* (1921).

M. Leumann 'Die lateinische Dichtersprache' *Museum Helveticum* 4 (1947) 117.

P. Maas quoted by Bailey 1757.

E. C. McCartney 'Modifiers that reflect the etymology of the words modified with special reference to Lucretius' *Classical Philology* 22 (1927) 184-200.

K. L. McKay 'Animals in war and ἰσονομία' *American Journal of Philology* 85 (1964) 125-6.

J. Martin *Titi Lucreti Cari De Rerum Natura* (1959)[4].

J. Masson *Lucretius: Epicurean and poet* vol. 1 (1907).

J. E. B. Mayor *Thirteen Satires of Juvenal* (1889)[4].

T. Mommsen *The History of Rome* translated by W. P. Dickson (1894) vol. 5, pp. 475-8.

G. Müller *Die Darstellung der Kinetik bei Lukrez* (1959).

H. A. J. Munro *T. Lucreti Cari De Rerum Natura* (1886)[4].

R. G. M. Nisbet *Cicero in Pisonem* 1961.

E. Norden *Virgil Aeneis* 6 (1957)[4] 438.

M. Pallottino *Etruscan Painting* (1952) 117, 127.

L. R. Palmer *The Latin Language* (1954) 106.

D. S. Parker *Epicurean Imagery in Lucretius De Rerum Natura* Diss. Princeton (1952) 43, 92.

C. Pascal *Il primo libro del De rerum natura* (1928).

A. S. Pease *Cicero De Natura Deorum* (1955-8).

R. Penrose *Picasso* (1958) 112.

J. Perret 'Le mythe de Cybèle' *Revue des études latines* 13 (1935) 343.

J. P. Postgate 'New light upon Lucretius' *Bulletin of the John Rylands Library* 10 (1926) 134-9.

H. Read *Collected Essays, Gerard Manley Hopkins* (1938) 147.

O. Regenbogen *Lukrez* (1932).

D. S. Robertson *A Handbook of Greek and Roman Architecture* (1945) 276.

Ronsard *L'Avant-venue du printemps*.

B. Roos 'Lucretius 2 150-2' *Mnemosyne* 20 (1967) 297-8.

W. H. D. Rouse *Lucretius De Rerum Natura* (1943).

M. Rozelaar *Lukrez* (1943) 67-72.

F. H. Sandbach 'Two passages in Lucretius' *Classical Review* 13 (1963) 13-14.

K. H. E. Schutter *Quibus annis comoediae Plautinae primum actae sint quaeritur* Diss. Groningen (1952) 28-9.

Shakespeare *Antony and Cleopatra* 4 12 2-9.

Sonnet 65.

Sonnet 73.

Shelley *Letter to Maria Gisborne* 35.

F. Solmsen 'Lucretius 1 724 and *Aetna* 1' *Classical Philology* 52 (1957) 251.

T. J. B. Spencer *Lucretius and the scientific poem in English* in Dudley 131 - 64.

G. J. Sullwold *Lucretius' Imagery: A poetic reading of the De Rerum Natura* Diss. Washington (1957).

Swift *On Dreams.*

Tennyson *The Two Voices* stanza 102.

J. H. Thiel 'De Lucretio puerorum vitae descriptore' *Mnemosyne* 58 (1930) 107.

S. Timpanaro junior 'Lucrezio 3 1' *Philologus* 104 (1960) 147-9.

Touring Club Italiano *L'Italia Fisica* plate 54, p. 96.

R. C. Trevelyan *Translations from Lucretius* (1920).

G. Townend *Imagery in Lucretius* in Dudley 95 -114.

P. Turner 'Shelley and Lucretius' *Review of English Studies* 10 (1959) 269 - 82.

G. Wakefield *Titi Lucretii Cari De Rerum Natura* (1813).

S. Weinstock 'Two archaic inscriptions from Latium' *Journal of Roman Studies* 50 (1960) 112 n9.

D. A. West 'Two notes on Lucretius' *Classical Quarterly* 14 (1964) 94-102.

E. C. Wickham *The Works of Horace* (1896)[3].

R. D. Williams *Virgil Aeneid* 5 (1960).

D. E. W. Wormell 'Lucretius: the personality of the poet'. *Greece and Rome* 7 (1960) 63.

The personal world of Lucretius in Dudley 35 - 68.

Appendix: Metaphor and Argument

A puzzle about the study of ancient Greek and Latin literature is that the mines are inexhaustible. They have been worked over for many centuries and still there are seams to be explored. One which seems promising to me is the function of metaphor in argument, as discussed in 1969 in the second chapter of this book. This appendix of 1994 is an attempt to point to some further possibilities in this area. Whether such enquiries will lead anywhere remains to be seen, but one thing is certainly true. This poet is worth reading and worth working at.

Lucretius says that he wishes in effect to touch the philosophy of Epicurus with the sweet honey of the Muses in order to retain the attention of the reader (1.936-50 = 4.11-25). His images are clearly an important part of this strategy, but that does not mean that they are extraneous ornaments. This book has shown throughout that the imagery supports the arguments, making them not only more vivid and memorable but also more cogent. This procedure shines out on every page of Lucretius and more could be done to show how it works. This appendix offers three examples.

¶ *The Procession of the Seasons (5.738-50).*[1] Why does the shape of the moon differ from night to night? Lucretius suggests four possibilities: either its light is reflected from the sun and its visible shape depends upon the nightly changes in the angle of reflection between sun, moon and earth; or else the moon has its own light but is masked in different ways night after night according to the position of an unseen body which glides along between the moon and the viewer on earth; or else because the moon is a sphere with a bright half and a dark half, showing us therefore a different form every night as it revolves; or else (and he keeps the most outrageous solution to the last) because a new moon is formed every 24 hours in a regular monthly rhythm whereby each night's moon is a little larger or smaller than its predecessor.

The explanation of this surprising form of argument is that Epicurean dogma held that the only use of natural science is to save us from fear of the heavenly bodies and of the gods (*Principal Doctrines* 11, *Letter to Pythocles* 85-7). Since we cannot know the truth about such matters, the important thing is to realise that there are possible material explanations. There is no need to believe that gods are responsible. Nor is there any need to agonise about the truth. Indeed, to hold to one belief as opposed to another is also a form of myth-making (*Letter to Pythocles* 87). It is perhaps in order to demonstrate the folly of such dogmatism that Lucretius keeps the most unlikely explanation of the phases of the moon to the last and devotes most space to it. Even the astounding theory of a new moon every night can be defended and Lucretius proceeds to defend it in 14 lines of glorious poetry. His argument is that it would be difficult to reject this theory because so many other things are created in a fixed order:

ordine cum <videas> tam certo multa creari.
it Ver et Venus et Veneris *prae*nuntius *ante*
pennatus graditur Zephyri *vestigia propter*,
Flora quibus mater *prae*spargens *ante* viai
cuncta coloribus egregiis et odoribus opplet.   740
inde loci sequitur Calor aridus et comes *una*
pulverulenta Ceres <et> etesia flabra Aquilonum.
inde Autumnus adit, graditur *simul* Euhius Euan.
inde aliae tempestates ventique secuntur,
altitonans Volturnus et Auster fulmine pollens.   745
tandem Bruma Nives adfert pigrumque Rigorem
reddit; Hiemps sequitur crepitans hanc dentibus algu.
quo minus est mirum si certo tempore luna
gignitur et certo deletur tempore rursus,
cum fieri possint tam certo tempore multa.[2]   750
    Lucretius 5.736-50

...since you see so many things created in a fixed order.
The Spring comes and Venus, and Venus' winged Herald
goes before them in the footprints of Zephyr,
while Flora, mother of flowers, sprinkles all the path
before them and fills the land with gorgeous colours and fragrances.
Next in order follows parching Heat and with him his companion
dusty Ceres and the etesian blasts of the Aquilones.
Next Autumn arrives and with him comes Euhius Euan.

Next follow other weathers and other winds,
high-thundering Volturnus and Auster mighty in his lightning.
At the last Shortest Day brings Snows and restores
sluggish Frost. Winter follows her, chattering her teeth with cold.
There is therefore no need to be surprised if a moon is created
at a fixed time, and at a fixed time again is destroyed,
since so many things can arise at fixed times.

The pageant is vividly described, a challenge to the mime artist. Typical of scenic or artistic descriptions in Latin poetry are the rich sound effects. We do not only see this procession before our eyes. We hear it going past. Cupid in 737 is a herald and heralds in classical antiquity were famous for the loudness of their voices. The next sounds we hear are the blasts of the etesian winds, the north-westers which blow in Italy in the Dog Days of high summer. Next, Autumn's companion Bacchus, busy with the vintage no doubt, is given his name based on the ritual cry *euoi! euoi!* Then more winds blow and in one of them the thunder is high-sounding because it is in the air, and also deep-sounding because of its low rumble (the Latin *altus* is usefully ambiguous, both 'high' and 'deep'). As the procession moves on, the sound of it dies away in the chattering of teeth.[3]

The passage is not only rich in auditory stimuli, it is also accurate, to a degree, as a description of the seasons. The first group is described in reverse order of arrival. First is Flora strewing her snowdrops and aconites before winter is over. Next come the warming western breezes which are followed closely by Cupid, the god of amorous desire, and then spring itself and Venus, the implementation of that desire. The summer scene is also realistic. Ceres, the goddess of grain is taking advantage of the hot, dry weather to get in the harvest and she is covered in dust from the winnowing floor.[4] Next, in the pageant and in real life, come autumn and the vintage, followed by a vital subdivision which allows the vintage to be over before the thunderstorms of late autumn begin. Last is most particular of all. The shortest day is December 21st and reasonably enough we can expect some snow around that date. But the real cold of winter is only then beginning.

These vivid and realistic details bring the description to life and make it cogent and memorable, but they are all tooled to support the argument. The argument as established at 736 and recapitulated at 748-50 gives clear indication of two salient points. The large number of different phenomena is declared at 736 and in the recap at 750 *(multa)*. Their fixed order is asserted at 732 before our extract begins *(ordine formarum certo certisque figuris)*, and again at 736 *(ordine certo)*, then three times more for all to hear in the recap with *certo tempore* at 748, 749 and 750 (West 1975).[5]

On the first point one might be anxious for Lucretius because there are only four seasons to correspond to the thirty days of the moon, but there is no need for anxiety. From the inexhaustible abundance of his imagination pours a procession with sixteen single participants as capitalised above and including Cupid from lines 737-8. The North Winds (the Aquilones), other winds and weathers of lines 742 and 744 and the Snows brought along by Winter comfortably make up the number. Second, the different shapes of each moon are represented by the vivid differentiation of the individual participants. They look different and they are engaged in strikingly different activities. At the head of the procession, for instance, the hint is that Flora is strewing flowers from her basket and, bringing up the rear, Frost, literally Stiffness, is sluggish because he is not quite managing to keep up with the others (like Quintus Fabius Maximus Cunctator, the Delayer, in Virgil *Aeneid* 6.845-6).[6] The fixed order of phenomena is established by reminders that this is a procession. This is achieved by repeated indications of place as italicised in the Latin and repeated verbs of movement. 'Following', for example, the verb *sequi*, is specifically asserted in lines 741, 744 and 747.

What makes the *De Rerum Natura* different from most other poetry is that Lucretius' material, like Bach's, is led by his argument, an argument passionately held and vigorously propounded. Other poets follow much more freely the promptings of their own intelligence, imagination and emotions.

¶ *Primitive Man and the Water Supply (5.945-52).* The food of primitive man was rough but abundant. He ate what Nature provided, acorns, anything that grew wild, in the winter arbutus berries. But how did he find water to drink?

at sedare sitim fluvii fontesque vocabant   945

ut nunc montibus e magnis decursus aquai
claru' citat late sitientia saecla ferarum.
denique nota vagi silvestria templa tenebant
nympharum, quibus e scibant umori' fluenta
lubrica proluvie larga lavere umida saxa,   950
umida saxa, super viridi stillantia musco
et partim plano scatere atque erumpere campo.
   2.945-52

But springs and rivers called upon him to slake his thirst
just as nowadays the rush of water down from high mountains
clearly summons the generations of wild beasts from far and wide.
And also in their wanderings they lived among familiar haunts
of Nymphs in the forests, from which they knew that gliding streams
of water washed the wet rocks with lavish flow,
washed the wet rocks, dripping over green moss,
and some flooded and burst over the level plain.

Again in this passage the poetry leaps to the eye and ear. In the first
three lines there is a lively personification as the rushing waters call
out to the thirsty, and the neat, double alliteration in 945 suits the sound
of rushing waters. But the poetic ornamentation is functional. The
double alliteration of line 945 locks the proposition to the analogy by
means of the similar double alliteration in line 947. The great mountains are not grandiose ornament but necessary to contrast with the
different scenes which follow and to explain the downrush of the
waters. We are on Speyside, not on the Fens. 'Clearly' *clarus* (947) is
a dazzling synaesthesia. The word is also used of sight. In the *Aeneid*
7.141-2 when Jupiter thundered clear from the heights, *clarus ab alto*
intonuit, scholars debate whether this is visual or aural. It seems that
Virgil is playing with both senses: Jupiter thunders loudly *and* from a
clear sky. If so Virgil may well have caught the idea from this passage
of Lucretius where the invitation of the waters is loud and clear, clear
as if it were a direct sighting.

   The five lines which follow have a notably lush poetic texture with
the liquid alliteration in line 950 and the endlessly repetitive gurgling
of water going over wet rocks in 950-1. These are not sound effects
for the sake of sound effects, but are all at work in the argument. There
are three main points: – men knew about the water (1), because they

lived in the woods and wandered about among them (2), and there was
an abundance of water flooding over at the springs and bursting out
on to the plains (3). The first two points are made immediately in *nota
vagi* which juxtaposes the wanderers with their knowledge of the
woodland haunts. Knowledge is stressed again in what follows since
they knew (*scibant*) that streams flowed from these haunts, of Dryads
and Naiads no doubt, the nymphs of woods and fountains. The flood
of alliteration and also the repeated laving of the rocks are functional
in that the inexhaustible *abundance* of the waters is necessary in order
to explain how they were found even though they were quiet.

So far so good. But there is a gap. What about (3), the plain
dwellers, far away from the mountains and the woodland springs, the
shrines of the Nymphs? This is the problem to which Lucretius now
addresses himself. *Partim* in line 952 'in part' is, as often, almost a
noun, 'some of it'. 'They knew that some of the water flooded over
stones and dripped over moss in the woods, and *some* overflowed and
burst out over distant plains'. The logic has swerved at this point.
Instead of explaining how plainsmen found water, he explains that
woodsmen knew how plainsmen found water – because there was
plenty of it in the plains. This may not be the simplest explanation of
this passage but from our present point of view the important point is
that *abundance* is a part of the argument. Plainsmen found water
because there was so much of it. This famous and highly wrought
passage is therefore a vivid and poetic description but, as ever, the
vividness and poetic details serve to make the teaching attractive and
memorable and they are also part of the argument.

¶ *Assimilation by Metaphor* (5.251-60). Lucretius argues from the
seen to the unseen, from the visible world to the invisible underlying
world of the atoms. The world as we know it will come to an end as
the atoms which constitute it separate and then reform in new arrangements. To prove this proposition Lucretius argues that if the parts of
a thing are perishable, are mortal, then the whole must be mortal. But
parts of our world are Earth, Air, Fire and Water. Earth, Air, Fire and
Water are mortal. Therefore our world is mortal.

principio pars terrai nonnulla, perusta
solibus assiduis, multa pulsata pedum vi,

pulveris exhalat nebulam nubesque volantis
quas validi toto dispergunt aere venti.
pars etiam glebarum ad diluviem revocatur
imbribus et ripas radentia flumina rodunt.
praeterea, pro parte sua, quod cumque alit auget,
redditur; et quoniam dubio procul esse videtur
omniparens eadem rerum commune sepulcrum.
ergo terra tibi libatur et aucta recrescit.

    5.251-60

First of all a fair amount of Earth, scorched
by unceasing suns and battered by the force of many feet,
breathes out a cloud of dust and flying vapours
which mighty winds disperse through all the air.
Some turf also is called back into the flood
by rain and scouring rivers gnawing away their banks.
Quite apart from that, whatever nourishes and gives increase,
is restored in due proportion, and since it seems to be beyond doubt
that the Mother of all things is also their common sepulchre,
therefore you must admit that the Earth trickles away (<u>libatur</u>)
                  and increases and grows again.

    The astonishing word is *libatur* in line 260, properly and commonly
used of liquids being poured or sipped. Although we have just read
that the Earth is eroded by Water, here Earth itself is imagined as being
poured away or sipped in the process of continual change. The
explanation is that Lucretius has slightly changed his argument. He is
no longer arguing simply that the four parts of our world are all mortal,
he is now explicitly arguing from lines 257-9 that they keep melting
away into each other. He sees this so vividly and is so eager to
represent it vividly that he actually speaks of Earth as though it were
Water, 'it is sipped, or trickles away' just as earlier, in line 253, it turned
into clouds and vapours. Lucretius has made his point in 257-8. He
now demonstrates it.

    This explanation is confirmed in the discussion of Water which
follows. Just as Earth is diminished by wind, sun and Water in 251-6,
so the abundance of Water in our world is kept in check by continuous
reductions as it is drawn off by wind, sun and underground seepage,
that is by Air, Fire and Earth:

sed primum quicquid aquai
tollitur in summaque fit ut nil umor abundet,
partim quod validi verrentes aequora *venti*
diminuunt radiisque retexens aetherius *sol*,
partim quod subter per *terras* diditur omnis.
    5.264-70

*...but every first particle of water is removed
and it comes about that in total water by no means superabounds,
partly because it is diminished by mighty winds sweeping the levels
of the sea and by the ethereal sun unweaving it with its rays,
partly because it seeps downwards under all the earth.*

Air is dealt with next. Here, in technical terms, there is a constant efflux of atoms from all objects into the air, but again we find assimilation by metaphor. The Air has become as Water;

semper enim quod cumque fluit de rebus, id omne
aeris in magnum fertur mare; qui nisi contra
corpora retribuat rebus recreetque fluentis,
omnia iam resoluta forent et in aera versa.
    5.275-8

*For always, whatever flows from objects, it is all
carried off into the great sea of air. If air in its turn
did not restore atoms to objects and recreate them as they flow
    away,
everything would already have been dissolved and turned into air.*

Fire also is assimilated to Water:

Largus item liquidi fons luminis, aetherius sol,
inrigat adsidue caelum candore recenti...
    5.281-2

*Similarly that fountain of liquid light, the ethereal sun,
ceaselessly waters the sky with brightness ever fresh...*

To sum up, Lucretius has no need to argue that Earth, Air, Fire and Water melt into one another. His original and essential point is that our world is mortal because its parts are mortal. In arguing throughout that the four parts are constantly diminished and decreased by each other and by speaking of Earth, Air and Fire as though they were Water, he is assimilating, by metaphor, different entities which, according to him, behave in similar ways. The effect of this procedure is exactly in line with his philosophy. He wishes further to destabilise our world. This pattern of thought is not unusual in Lucretius. His message is that our visible world is made up of minute, invisible atoms. To establish this, he argues to the unseen atoms from visible analogies, from the specks of dust swirling in a ray of sunlight to the unresting rearrangement of atomic particles. So intensely does he visualise his analogy, so insistently does he wish to enforce it on his readers that analogy on occasion is presented as identity. This confusion between resemblance and identity is seen in various forms in *De Rerum Natura*, notably on pages 41-6 and 89-91, most vividly perhaps in the passage discussed on pages 99-100 above where the confusion is so reckless that scholars still shy away from it. For Lucretius, Tityos the giant suffering eternal torment in the underworld in 3.984-94, does not exist. Tityos is the lover lying there with birds tearing at him, anxiety and anguish gnawing away at him and cares rending his flesh. Of course scholars are right. Birds do not tear at the entrails of lovers. But because Lucretius sees the analogy so starkly and wishes us to see it with equal vividness he allows the analogy to creep into the reality. Birds do eat the entrails of lovers in Lucretius. There is no need to alter the manuscript reading and no need to think of the pretty arrows of winged Hellenistic Cupids.[7] The visible world is used to prove the invisible truth and at times the two merge.

References
Page 136[1]. A more discursive treatment of this passage in Tzifopoulos and West (1991).
Page 137[2]. In this appendix as in the body of the book, I use the text of J. Martin (1957) except for the punctuation of 738 and the capitals in lines 742 and 746. At 5.947 I read *claru' citat* for his *claricitat*, which gives an inappropriate sense, and at 949 *umori'* for his *umore*.
Page 138[3]. For sound effects in an ekphrasis at Virgil *Aeneid* 5.253-5, see West (1993). Not that Lucretius' pageant of the seasons is an ekphrasis. Commentators are too ready to suggest that poets are imitating artists, as though poets had no visual imagination. No Roman painting was like this.
Page 138[4]. The first four feet of the dactylic hexameter are combina-

tions of dactyls (-uu) and spondees (—). In the 1457 lines of this fifth book of the *De Rerum Natura* 26 begin with four dactyls, one in every 56 lines. When three of these occur consecutively here in 740-2, and another three consecutively in 499-501, cited on page 116, a passage describing the lightness and purity of the *aether*, we should be hearing the poetry. P.M. Brown, xliii n.65, draws attention to the effect of contrast between polyspondaic and polydactylic lines at 1.662-3 and 1003-4. Compare 5.392-4.

Page 139[5]. For reprise technique see West (1975).

Page 139[6]. For *quo fessum rapitis?* see West in *Tria Lustra*, forthcoming.

Page 144[7]. For Cupids see Kenney on 3.992-4 (1971) and more fully (1970).

Works mentioned in the Preface and Appendix

P.M. Brown *Lucretius De Rerum Natura I* (1984).

R.D. Brown *Lucretius on Love and Sex* (1987).

C.J. Classen 'Poetry and Rhetoric in Lucretius' *TAPA* 99 (1968) 77-118, reprinted in Classen (1986).

    (ed.), *Probleme der Lukrezforschung* (1986).

D. Clay *Lucretius and Ehicurus* (1983).

C.D.N. Costa *Lucretius De Rerum Natura V* (1984).

I. Dionigi *Lucrezio. Le parole e le cose* (1988).

J. Godwin *Lucretius: De Rerum Natura IV* (1985).

H.B. Gottschalk *CP* 70 (1975) 42-4.

E.J. Kenney 'Doctus Lucretius' *Mnemosyne* 23 (1970) 366-92.

    Lucretius (1977) available from the Honorary Treasurer of the Classical Association, Richard Wallace, Classics, The University, Keele, ST5 5BG (£4 to members, £6.50 to non-members, inclusive of postage).

    'Tityos and the Lover' *PCPS* 16 (1970) 44-7.

    Lucretius De Rerum Natura III (1971).

A.A. Long and D.N. Sedley *The Hellenistic Philosophers*, 2 vols with bibliography in vol. 2.476-512.

M.F. Smith *Lucretius De Rerum Natura* (1975), a revision of Rouse's Loeb translation.

J.M. Snyder, *Puns and Poetry in Lucretius* De Rerum Natura (1980).

Y. Tzifopoulos 'Lucretius on the Seasons' *Hellenica* 38 (1988) 401-5.

D. West 'Lucretius' Methods of Argument' *CQ* 25 (1975) 94-116.

review of Snyder in *CR* 32 (1982) 25-7.

'The Rite of Spring in Lucretius 5.720-50' *Renaissance Studies* 5 (1991) 242-9.

review of Dionigi in *Gnomon* 63 (1991) 647-9.

'On Serial Narration and on the Julian Star' *Proceedings of the Virgil Society* 21 (1993) 4.

'The Pageant of the Heroes as Panegyric' in *Tria Lustra* edited by H.D. Jocelyn (forthcoming).

Index of Ancient Authors

Names in brackets after an author indicate that the author in brackets is being quoted.

Index of Modern Authors

Index of Passages in Lucretius